No Ordinary Spy

A Novel By Jack Petro

Second Edition

1stBooks – rev. 07/09/03

Acknowledgments

Many thanks to Esther McBride, Dick Marshall, Marcia Foxell, Diana Harned, and Joe Dieglio who provided the suggestions, editing, and encouragement needed to keep me writing. Also thanks to my wife, Jan, who initiated and planned the trips for us to research the European locations.

CHAPTER ONE

There was little activity at the traffic circle just a half-mile east the Arc de Triomphe. It was early Saturday morning and Paris was slow in awakening from the hangover wrought by the excesses of a spring Friday night. Antoine stood at a newsstand where he paid for a newspaper while keeping an eye on a well-dressed man with a small brown briefcase approaching the *pisswaire* some 100 yards away. He turned so he faced the public rest stop and leaned against a light pole as he feigned interest in an article.

Another figure entered his view from the south. Henry Winston had been dropped off by a car less than a half mile away. He was casually dressed and also had a small brown briefcase. Antoine was expecting him. Winston strolled to the outdoor rest room where Antoine watched the feet of the two men. They stopped at a distance from each other with their toes pointing outward. Then the first man moved briskly past the other, exited the stall, and resumed walking in his initial direction. After a measured pause, Winston emerged making his way south where he had arranged for his driver to pick him up.

Antoine was already in position. When Winston exited, he was just a few feet behind.

He drew his automatic pistol placing the newspaper over it as he jammed it into Winston's back.

"Keep walking, Monsieur Winston. Do not think of being a hero. I know you have a gun so keep your hands where I can see them. Go right at the first street. We are going for a walk in the park this morning."

Antoine knew more about Winston than just his name. He had been given a complete dossier through a leak at the American Embassy in London. Winston was Ivy League, majoring in Romance Languages. The CIA recruited him over a year ago. After a course in covert operations, he assumed courier duties at the American Embassy as his initial assignment. He was particularly useful in France, Spain, and Italy where he spoke the languages fluently. He was single, dated occasionally, was very precise in his assignments, and did not drink excessively. Paris was a frequent stop for couriers and Antoine had shadowed him several times.

At first Winston was totally surprised but remained calm. He then realized that the choice of the *pisswaire* for the drop was a huge mistake. It had given cover to the approach of his assailant. The car was nowhere in sight, but he had a strategy. This was not a simple robbery. His adversary knew his name, so he must be an agent probably working for the USSR. No special instructions been given on the importance of the pickup briefcase, so there was no need to risk his life to protect its contents. He would remain calm, stall for time, and hope that his companions in the car would spot him. Even if he did surrender the briefcase, there was a good chance the three of them could stop the agent before he got very far.

Antoine had his own plan. He prodded Winston to quicken his step as the Bois de Boulogne loomed in front of them. The park quickly engulfed them. The spring growth of trees and shrubs had not yet been trimmed and the rays of the morning sun were muted.

The path they took ended in a small lake where rowboats were rented. It was much too early for the boat stall to be open. The area was deserted. Without a word, the force of the pistol pushed Winston onto the boat pier until he was within three yards of the end.

"Stop, Monsieur Winston. Slowly drop the briefcase."

Winston became uneasy. The man could have taken the briefcase from him at any time, taken his gun, then walked away. The package was the important thing, not the courier. Something was wrong. He decided it was time to turn.

Antoine was prepared. He already had his foot raised and smashing it into Wilson's midsection drove him off the pier and into the water. The feeding waterfowl raised a ruckus. The briefcase skidded along the pier and he stopped it with his foot. He was in no hurry to get to the end of the pier. Winston's dossier noted that he was a poor swimmer. The well-planned kick to the solar plexus expelled the air from his lungs, forcing him to inhale water as he plunged in.

Shear instinct brought Winston frantically thrashing to the surface. Gasping for breath, he started to move toward the dock. Antoine quickly grabbed an oar from one of the boats and swung it squarely into Winston's head. The swimmer quietly sank as blood tinted the water

Antoine looked around. The ducks were settling down. No sign of anything else moving. He retrieved the briefcase. Following instructions, he removed a single sheet of paper, folded it and placed it in his pocket. He tore the few remaining pages into small pieces and dumped them into a nearly full trash bin at the end of the dock. The empty briefcase would go in the next trash receptacle.

The agent took a few moments to look over the pond to be sure Winston did not somehow reappear. He still felt remorse each time he had to kill during his ten-year span of covert action, but it was part of the job. Eliminating Winston was an essential piece of a plan to cripple communications out of America's London Embassy by removing several low echelon players. The first courier had been turned with money now living the good life in a Central American country. Winston's record indicated that neither the dollar, drugs, nor sex would be sufficient temptation, so more drastic action was called for. Timing it to the live drop with the Russian turncoat was simply opportunistic.

Antoine took his time strolling through the park exiting on its extreme southern end. He would contact the Soviet embassy in the afternoon. By then the Russian would have been apprehended with a briefcase full of money and the paper he retained would be sufficient to sentence him to Siberia at the least. In addition the CIA Station in London would be caught without a single courier.

* * *

It was the spring of 1953 and the war in Korea was at a stalemate. The Chinese had dug in close to the 38th parallel. Truce talks were going on, but the U.S. was wary of another Chinese onslaught. They vastly outnumbered the UN forces, and another series of human wave attacks could prove demoralizing. All

U.S. military and intelligence resources were focused on the Far East.

In Europe, the Russians viewed the preoccupation of NATO's leader as an opportunity to add some temperature to the cold war. A return to the Blockade of Berlin was an option, but an invasion of West Germany using the *Volkspolizei*, the armed East German police force, seemed more likely. An outright invasion of the European continent by Russian troops was not out of the question. The Russians must move soon or lose their momentary field advantage.

Lt. James C. Parker, Communications and Cryptographic Officer of the USS Perry, sat in the ship's radio shack as the destroyer cruised in formation with the Sixth Fleet in the middle of the Mediterranean Sea. It was Sunday morning and the flotilla was proceeding at a leisurely 12 knots through a mirror smooth sea.

The duty radioman had his earphones on and sat with his feet up on a table. Lt. Parker was waiting for the morning newssheet. He routinely took it to the Wardroom so his fellow officers could have something to debate during breakfast. He ran his hand over the cold steel edge of the table that held the Teletype then onto the machine. It was warm and friendly by comparison. It was his window to the outside world and broke the boredom of a ship at sea. The Teletype began to click. He leaned over. It wasn't the news update. It was Priority Urgent FOX clear language, calling for immediate attention but not critical enough to be encrypted. The message was simple:

> All Com 6th Fleet
> Dispatch to London Embassy most Senior Junior Officer with Top Secret Clearance on current non-critical assignment. TAD
> Immediate

The morning news would have to wait that Sunday.

It took only 97 minutes for Parker to be identified. He had served in the Navy for two years as an enlisted man at the end of WWII. When being discharged, a recruiter tweaked his patriotic button and talked him into signing up for a 4-year hitch in the reserves. The GI Bill made going to college a financial cakewalk for him. Six years later, a telegram arrived. "Report to active duty." When the Korean War began, President Harry S. Truman had extended all reserve enlistments and hadn't bothered to let Parker know.

With a college degree in hand, Parker was offered and accepted an immediate commission, borrowed a uniform from a college fraternity brother, and headed for his assignment on a destroyer based in Norfolk, Virginia. With a serial number going back to 1945, he technically had been a Lieutenant for eight years. No other junior officer in the 6th Fleet was even close in seniority.

Two hours later Parker stood at ease before Commander Keiffer in the wardroom of DD-697.

"Looks like you've drawn some sort of special Temporary Additional Duty in London. Hate to lose you, but I had no choice," Keiffer lied as he signed the orders. An Academy man, he roiled at being stuck with so many Reserve Officers. Assigned to the Mediterranean when the real action was in the Far East just added to his frustrations.

Keiffer folded the papers and placed them in a jacket. He looked up. Parker was of average height and weight and in reasonably good physical condition. His sandy hair and light complexion made him look younger than his 25 years. He took his responsibilities as Communications Officer seriously and was a fairly good Officer of the Deck during Combat Readiness Drills, but tended to be flippant in the face of authority. He had a sloppy salute and never seemed to be standing up straight. No, not a gentleman and definitely not anything near Academy caliber. Glad to get rid of him.

"We'll arrange transportation as soon as we dock in Naples."

From Naples to London the weather was crystal clear. Parker was the only passenger on the twin engine Convair. Once they reached cruising altitude he got a view of the Alps he never imagined. The sharpened image of the snow-capped peaks stood out against the bright blue sky.

It was also a long way from Cleveland, Ohio, where he was raised. Most of what he could remember about growing up was fashioned by the Great Depression. His mother was divorced and raised him and an older sister in the toughest of times when it was not fashionable to be a single mother. There was never enough to eat; yet he couldn't remember being hungry. Maybe it was a conditioned response. With money scarce, keeping up with the rent was a struggle. Eviction came every six months or so and they changed schools more than a dozen times. James adapted better than his sister. He made friends easily, but never got really close to anyone knowing the next separation was not far away.

A new kid on the block, he was a ready-made target for bullies but he quickly learned how to hold his own. Although slight of build, he offset his smaller size by his agility and quick wits making him a dangerous opponent. He had survived the Depression and, though not necessarily better for it, he had been tempered by it.

"You must be pretty important to rate a private plane." The pilot relaxed and removed his cap. "They even told me to be sure you wore a parachute on the entire flight," he chuckled.

"Yeah," Parker mused. "Am I lucky, or what?"

The U. S. Embassy in London was easy to find. A doorman ushered him in. Once inside, Parker extended his papers towards the Marine guard in full dress uniform. The guard snapped to attention and saluted. Parker shifted the papers to his left hand as quickly as he could to return the salute. It left him slightly off balance and looking like a clod. The guard graciously appeared not to notice, then glanced briefly at the papers. "Down the hall, sir, third door on the left," he directed as he saluted again. This saluting is becoming a pain in the ass, he thought.

The first few doors had the usual signs: *Deputy Ambassador, Public Relations, Records.* The third on the left had no sign. Maybe the GI-rine was mistaken, Parker guessed. He glanced back. One, two, three. No mistake there. He tried the door. It was locked. Before his hand left the knob, a buzzer sounded and the door opened. The room was not vacant.

"We keep it locked. Too many people think this is the loo."

Parker was surprised by the British accent here at the Embassy. The voice came from a trim, smartly dressed woman behind the desk, the sole piece of furniture in the room. Her hair was pulled back tightly and her black rimmed glasses announced she was all business. He guessed she was in her mid forties and probably had great legs.

"I'm Penelope Davenport, Security Administrative Assistant. You must be Parker".

Parker smiled and handed her his papers. He liked the way she drew out both r's in his name. Davenport gave them a cursory glance and set them down. "Do you know what your assignment is?"

"'Aven't the foggiest," Parker quipped in his best try at a British accent. Davenport raised an eyebrow and pursed her lips.

"You'll be attached to the Embassy," she began her explanation. "You will be transporting classified materials and," she added in a more measured pace, "be given some miscellaneous assignments. Since you will be traveling a great deal, we've arranged for a room at the Wellington Arms Residential Hotel. Modest, but comfortable. Our driver will take you there to show you the way. After that you'll be on your own."

Without rising, she handed him a sheet of paper. "This is your schedule for the next three days. Take a look and see if there are any questions."

Saturday:	Queen's Ball at Windsor
	Dress Whites, Black Tie
Sunday:	Lunch with Prince Philip on the Royal Racing Yacht
	Reception, Dinner at Coat of Arms Restaurant, Isle of Wight
	Dress Blues, Staff Braid
Monday:	Report to Embassy Security, Basement
	0800 civilian clothes

Parker reflected on his good fortune. "Looks great!"

"We're still celebrating the Coronation, you know," Davenport pointed out.

"So I've heard."

"You'll have the opportunity to meet some of our colleagues at these functions. You start work Monday. And, we must get you a new uniform," she added managing to get in a jab.

Parker looked down at his uniform.

"It's too scruffy for Embassy staff."

Parker was caught off guard. Scruffy? He had worked long and hard getting the braid tarnished enough to get a modest measure of respect from the enlisted men. Salty, maybe, but not scruffy.

Davenport interrupted his thoughts, "American size 44 Regular?"

Parker sucked in his gut and stood up straighter. "Try 42 regular," he retorted trying to get even.

"We'll send a new uniform to the hotel tonight with staff braid so you can be presentable over the weekend. Only four ribbons. Hmmm, I'll review your service record and see if we can legitimately add a few more to make you respectable." Davenport scored the touché as she rose from the desk.

"Welcome to the Embassy", she said extending her hand while showing him the door.

He'd been right about one thing: great legs.

By 0900 Monday morning, Davenport had finished briefing Parker on security procedures at the Embassy.

"I've put together a chart of the organization," she said coming around from behind her desk. Standing, she placed the paper on the desk in front of Parker and leaned forward. "The Ambassador is on top, obviously. Don't pay much attention to the titles," she pointed to the names running down the sheet. "Captain Foxworthy is the ranking officer of the Naval Attaché which includes the Marine contingent. You are in Commander Smythe's group which handles communications and security at this location."

"So I'm here," Parker said pointing to a blank area at the bottom of the page. He was savoring the early morning scent of a well-scrubbed woman.

"That's where the junior officers dwell," she replied. She straightened up. "The Marines want to see you for some fire arms review." She headed for the door and Parker had to move quickly to keep up with her.

The next thirty minutes Parker was given the quickest drill on the use of a pistol in the annals of

11

Naval History. The Marine barked and motioned instructions. Parker's training as an enlisted man did not cover the use of side arms. The Marine was not at all pleased with his student.

In a room next to the firing range Chief Petty Officer Higgins stood in front of Parker, slipping a clean Government Issue .45 into the shoulder holster he had just fitted on the young lieutenant. "Be careful. There's a shell in the chamber plus a full clip. Keep the safety on or you'll shoot your foot off," CPO Higgins warned. Parker made a mental note. The gunner's mate rating and three rows of combat ribbons had made their impression on him.

Parker put on his suit coat. "I can barely button this. Look at this bulge." The weight and size of the gun under his coat made him feel uncomfortable.

Higgins gave a quick look. "Bring the coat in early tomorrow morning and I'll have the Embassy tailor make some quick alterations. For now, just hunch over a bit when you go in to see the boss."

Resenting the chief's self-assured, somewhat condescending attitude, Parker figured he'd probably gone through this routine before. "Just what am I supposed to do with this gun?" he challenged.

"When the time comes, you'll know...you'll know," Higgins replied with a cynical half smile. "I saw you on the range. You set a record. Three clips and never hit the target."

Parker scowled and shook his head. It wasn't his idea to enroll in a crash pistol course.

"Don't be too concerned," Higgins continued as he read the facial expression. "Most of the recruits are lousy shots. You'll probably hit something if it's closer than 10 feet. Farther than that, you'll scare the bastards off with the noise."

"I hear you met up with the captain Saturday night at Windsor," the chief continued as he made a final adjustment to the suit coat minimizing the bulge of the gun. "He's expecting you at ten sharp so you'd better get topside on the double." As Parker left, Higgins shook his head mumbling to himself. "Where do they get these fish? This one looks like he needs help tying his shoe laces."

Captain Amos J. Foxworthy was a balding, fiftyish Line Officer who was not pleased with the London assignment. A fleet officer passed over without explanation, he was a long way from Admiral…. maybe never. Under Foxworthy's direction the naval attaché group was known as a no-nonsense organization. He ran it as if he were still on the bridge of the cruiser he loved so well. The niceties, protocol, and parties were, for him, just penance for some wrong, long forgotten action in his past. Recently divorced, he had little in the way of diversion and approached his daily five-mile jog through Hyde Park with a vengeance. The rigorous schedule kept him in excellent physical condition, which was accented by his taste for sharply tailored uniforms.

Foxworthy informally met Parker in the Embassy Limo on the way to the Queen's Ball at Windsor. At the celebration, the Captain took time to introduce Parker to other Embassy personnel and some important British contacts. Between cocktails, he gave Parker a curt and to the point briefing: He had been selected solely on the basis of his rank, serial number, and Top Secret Clearance. The Embassy was aware Parker had no training for this assignment, but was caught short and needed a courier replacement ASAP. A hostess gliding towards them with a young woman in tow was a signal to end the conversation. He'd fill the rest in Monday.

The hostess and Foxworthy exchanged greetings. She turned towards Parker. "Stephanie is just dying to dance, Lieutenant?"

"My pleasure," Parker replied. He took her hand and headed for the dance floor.

"Do you know the quick step?" she asked.

"No, but I'm a quick study," Parker answered with a smile looking down at the face of his comely dance partner.

The Spartan furnishings in Foxworthy's office reflected England's state of recovery from World War II. Candy, coffee, and meat were still rationed and industry was just rebuilding from the devastation wrought by the German bombers. The pre-war mahogany desk was flanked by the perfunctory U.S. Flag. An artist's rendition of the cruiser, Chicago, in combat readiness with battle ribbons beneath hung on the back wall. A small table and four wooden chairs used as a conference area completed the furnishings.

Precisely at 1000, Parker entered the office, came to attention, and rendered one of his better salutes. "Reporting for duty, sir."

"At ease Parker, no need to salute around here when you're out of uniform." Foxworthy said with some disdain. "Did you enjoy yourself on the Royal Racing Yacht?"

"It was great. I know where some of the best gin in England is served. Philip was really down-to-earth when it came to naval matters." He barely was able to refrain from adding 'Philip was a real prince,' but he had been warned by staff not to stretch the captain's sense of humor.

"I expected that you'd have enjoyed the weekend, but now you have to earn your keep. Your basic assignment is to carry codes and classified documents to other embassies in Europe as well as to the Flag Admiral of the Sixth Fleet. You'll wear a uniform and a side arm and carry diplomatic credentials. Occasionally you'll be in civilian clothes to make some very routine drops and retrievals from agents on the continent." Foxworthy paused studying Parker's questioning expression.

"Is this sort of like 'Foreign Intrigue' where you have a brief case handcuffed to your wrist?" Parker asked, holding up his left fist.

"Not exactly. We changed the system some time ago. You will never be carrying a complete code at any one time, so although compromising a single delivery would be embarrassing, it would not be critical." Looking straight at Parker and without changing his tone he added, "We lost too many wrists."

Parker knew this was no joke. A flash of perspiration trickled down his back and his left arm twitched. Maybe he wasn't as lucky as he'd thought.

Foxworthy quickly changed the subject. "Here are some passports, driver's licenses, and other documents you will be needing. For money and miscellaneous items see Davenport."

Parker picked up the passports. The pictures were his, but he gaped in disbelief. "There must be a mistake. These all have different names."

"You need to change documents on certain assignments so you are not easily identified when going through immigration. It's best for you and the Service."

There was a definite pause in the conversation. Parker's brain was spinning. He had a sensation of going down for the second time.

Foxworthy filled the void. "Commander Smythe will give you your assignment tomorrow morning. We have a simple retrieval for you to make in Munich on Wednesday. You will be wearing civilian clothes and carrying a .45. Higgins gave you instructions, didn't he?"

"Yes sir, but I haven't had much experience with a .45." Parker frowned. "Just what am I supposed to do with the gun?"

"When the time comes, you'll know," Foxworthy replied in a fatherly tone. "Any other questions?"

"I was wondering, sir, where are the other couriers? I didn't meet any at the party at Windsor or on the yacht."

"Well, I explained that we were short. That's why you were transferred so quickly. Normally two are sufficient, but we like to have three."

Parker paused for a moment then succumbed to an old nervous habit of shifting his position in his seat. "Where are the other two?"

"They're lost," Foxworthy replied almost matter-of-factly.

"Lost? How could they be lost?" Tension etched lines in Parker's face.

"Well, it's just that we can't find them, that's all. It happens from time to time, but it's unusual to lose two almost at the same time. Sooner or later we find them. You have a definite advantage. No one knows you and you know nothing. Relax. We don't expect to lose you."

Foxworthy needed to end this conversation. "Report to Commander Smythe at 0900 tomorrow for your assignment. And see if you can do something about that coat. It looks like you're carrying a loaf of bread in your armpit. That will be all, Lieutenant."

Parker left, shaking his head. *I don't even have a will. Nobody gets "lost". Someone helped them get "lost". How do they "find" them? Dead? Alive? In pieces?* His head was buzzing as he passed by the Marine guard. He needed to get to the Wellington to clear his mind. The Embassy doorman called for the limousine to pull up. Suddenly he felt sick. The doorman had only one arm. Why hadn't he noticed that on the way in?

CHAPTER TWO

The callboard at Heathrow flashed. The British Overseas Airway 5 PM flight to Munich was in the process of boarding. Parker moved quickly through customs and passport control. No problem. His newly tailored suit coat almost perfectly concealed the .45 nestled in the holster over his left shoulder. No one seemed to bother to give him a second look.

Earlier when Davenport handed him his ticket, the first class status came as a surprise. "We like our new people to start off in style." Then she added, "Good luck."

Parker quickly checked the documents and counted out his German mark cash advance. The passport and the tickets had matching names, not his. Catching Davenport's eye, Parker said, "Well, everything checks. See you tomorrow."

Davenport smiled, but didn't answer.

"The mission is a routine retrieval," Commander Jeffery Smythe had told him during the briefing. "You fly into Munich on a late afternoon flight. Check into the Torbrau Hotel on Tal Strasse. Go to the Hofbrauhaus on Am Platzl. It's about three blocks away and is the largest beer hall in Munich. You'll have no trouble finding it. Your contact will meet you at 2235 exactly. Sit in the bench against the farthest wall from the door. The contact has a complete description of you and will sit as directly across from you as possible. You will be offered a cigarette. Your response will be 'Thanks, I've been trying to quit for five months but no luck.' You will be handed the pack of cigarettes. Take one out, light it."

Parker interrupted, "I don't smoke."

"Well, you'd better learn before tonight," Smythe continued. "Keep the cigarettes in front of you. The contact will have a beer and leave. Pick up the cigarettes then leave after an appropriate time. Do not leave the cigarettes out of your sight. Sleep with them if you have to, but bring them back here tomorrow directly from the airport."

"Oh, by the way, don't bother to look inside the pack," Smythe added. "It's better for you if you don't know what you're transporting."

* * *

Parker leaned back in his first class seat. Not bad, he thought. At least he was traveling in style. Maybe he could con Davenport into getting him first class on future assignments. Maybe he could be nice to her, maybe he could......and he dozed off.

"Anything to drink?" the stewardess asked.

"What?" Parker was still in a daze from his nap.

"Would you like a cocktail?"

"Just a Coke, please." Parker thought it better to keep a clear head on his first assignment.

"A gin and lime," a very British reply came from the next seat.

Parker had asked for the smoking section so he could experiment with the cigarettes he'd picked up at the airport. He lighted up painstakingly, holding the cigarette between his thumb and index finger. His little finger seemed to straighten involuntarily. He drew a deep breath through the cigarette and coughed twice before he gained control of himself. The co-passenger moved slightly away from him. A stealthy glance revealed that the Brit held his cigarette with his first two fingers and remaining digits firmly tucked into his palm. Parker switched his hold as discretely as possible. The Brit noticeably relaxed.

The flight was uneventful. Carrying only a small suitcase, Parker was waved through customs and passport control. He pitched the pack of Parliaments in the trash. He had experimented enough.

Though the Hofbrauhaus was within walking distance of the hotel, Parker thought it was his duty to take a taxi and spend some of the German marks that Davenport had given him. Besides, he wanted to try out his high school German. The hotel doorman never gave him a chance. He took charge, gave the driver the destination and extended his hand for a tip.

The *oom pah pah oom pah pah* music streamed out from the beer hall. Parker was amazed by its size. Long tables with benches were arranged with German-like precision. It was nearly filled and he guessed that close to a thousand people were there. It was just about 10 PM and it was obvious most everyone was well past the first beer. The band had everyone swaying back and forth. *Eins... Zwie... Drie....* and something else Parker could not make out. The hall, perfectly described by Smythe, made him feel at ease. He sidestepped through the waitresses carrying five steins in each hand until he reached the back wall and slid onto the bench.

As the brass band paused briefly between songs, the ten occupants of the table resumed their love affairs with beer.

"Willkomen," came from his left.

"Guten abend. Wie Geht es," Parker replied in his best German. Miss Weiss at Lincoln High would be proud of him, he thought.

"*Amerikanisch.* Ve speak gut English. Haf a beer. Ve haf plenty."

A stein came sliding toward Parker and magically stopped directly in front of him.

"Danke." Parker needed to get in at least a little practice German.

"You can buy der next roundt."

Parker should have known there was a catch to that free beer. He looked around. Where was the contact? Judging by their casual dress, he guessed most of the customers were locals. Maybe 30 or 40 were in business attire and probably half of these were most likely foreign visitors or businessmen. Anyone of them could be the contact. He had done his part; all he had to do now was wait.

It was 10:45 on Parker's watch. Ten minutes late. They never told him how long to wait. Suddenly panic clouded his mind. *He was about to screw up his first assignment. He was in the wrong place. He misunderstood Smythe's instructions. He got the time wrong.* The room got very hot. He began to sweat. *Was it the beer? Was it poisoned? Was this how the others were "lost"?* As panic increased its grip, a woman from the next table took the seat opposite him. She had obviously been at the tavern for some time and came with beer in hand, joining in the singing with the others at the table.

Oh God! Parker thought. *She took the contact's seat! How the hell am I going to get her out of there?* He sat motionless. He grasped for something to say, but his high school German suddenly abandoned him.

The music stopped. Parker studied the woman. She didn't seem to know the others at his table, but obviously had no trouble fitting in at this hour of the evening. Her plain skirt and loose fitting colored blouse were commonplace. She wasn't particularly attractive, but had a trim figure with the standard *Fraulien* D cup. She turned toward Parker. "You vant a cigarette?" she asked offering him the pack.

"I don't smoke," he replied without thinking. The woman continued holding out the cigarettes while looking straight into his eyes for what seemed an eternity. Her expression did not change. Parker's mind went numb for a second, then quickly shifted from park into overdrive. "That's not true," Parker said, shaking his head. "I've been trying to quit for five months, but I haven't had any luck. I'll have one."

She slid a pack of Camels across the table. Parker lit up as best he could. The music started again. The man on Parker's left put his arm over Parker's shoulder and locked him into swaying with the rest of the table before he could even put his hand over the cigarettes. He grabbed them on the second sway, but by that time the woman was gone.

Two beers later, Parker decided it was time to go. *"Auf Widersehen,"* he hailed the group, peeling off enough marks for the next round and making his way to the exit. He began to feel good about himself. Not bad for his first assignment. This was easier than he thought.

He looked for a taxi, but there were none. The hotel was just three blocks away so he started off on foot, one of only a few pedestrians.

The Germans had done a remarkable job rebuilding Munich. From the shambles of May 1945, most of the city was cleaned up and the center of the town was nearly restored. It was dark, very dark. Electric power was still in short supply so the streetlights were routinely turned off at 11 PM.

Parker turned left on Am Platzl and took another sharp left on a small street that crossed to Tal Strasse. Only darkened shops and an occasional office building lined the street.

As the songs from the Hofbrauhaus faded, rapidly approaching footsteps broke the descending silence. Parker turned, but too late. Caught off balance, he was pushed into an unlighted entrance way, his back to the wall. Blocking his way was a young man now silhouetted against any remaining light from the street. *"Geben mich euer geldtasche!"* His request was reinforced by the glint of a knife blade.

Parker stiffened. Trying to discourage him, be blurted *"Ich bin ein Amerikaner."* That was a big, big mistake.

"Giff me your vallet," the young man added with a smirk. He had cornered a good catch for the night.

Parker reached in his rear pants pocket, grasping his wallet. It wasn't his money. Probably counterfeit anyway, so give the kid the dough and get back to the hotel.

The young man made a tossing motion. Parker obliged with the wallet.

"Giff me your cigarettes!"

Parker broke into a cold sweat. American cigarettes were worth a lot more than the damn marks in the wallet. His first mission was about to go down the tubes. This brief reflection on his lack of intellect was broken by voices. A small group of Germans singing songs from the Hofbrauhaus was approaching the building. As they neared, the man took one step toward Parker, blocking his opportunity to escape. When they passed, the man repeated the demand: "Cigarettes, *schnell!"* He moved even closer.

Obligingly, Parker's right hand reached across to the shoulder holster in almost a casual manner as if to retrieve his cigarettes and gave the thief a shoulder shrug with a 'What do I care look.' The man impatiently motioned with his outstretched hand. Parker's grip closed on the .45 as the knife came within inches. Higgins' words about what to do with the gun rang in his ear...."you'll know, you'll know." Suddenly, he knew.

CHAPTER THREE

What happened next was locked in Parker's memory as a ballet in slow motion. Actually the entire incident was over in three seconds. The pistol easily came out of the holster and Parker swept it in a backhanded motion toward the middle of his assailant's face. The man's eyes widened with surprise and, with the agility of youth, he stepped back and ducked. But the barrel of the pistol caught him in the temple.

The young man continued back a step and almost simultaneously, the knife dropped, his eyes closed, and blood gushed from his forehead. His body went limp and fell forward, brushing Parker as he collapsed.

Parker looked down. Just a kid and a lucky one, he reasoned, since in the panic Parker couldn't remember where the safety was. He bent down closer to retrieve his wallet and felt his own breath coming in short heavy bursts. He could hear his pulse as if his heart was suddenly in his head. It was time to go. He swallowed deeply to gain control of himself.

A quick look showed that the street was empty. Parker had only one thought in mind. Get out of there as fast as he could and back to the hotel. Even though his mind was clear and the motivation strong, Parker couldn't move faster than a stroll. The harder he tried, the more slowly he seemed to walk. As he stopped for a moment to gather his wits, the problem registered in a flash. He looked down. His knees were shaking so badly; he was lucky to still be standing. Taking a long deep breath, he continued toward the hotel as best he could.

Sitting erect, Captain Foxworthy arranged several papers on his desk so that they resembled a flotilla. He then picked up his desk pen. Turning it around, he began to impatiently drum on the mahogany trim.

Commander Smythe sat slouched in one of the chairs taking a noisy sip from his morning cup of tea. The commander appeared to be the complete antithesis of Foxworthy. He was grossly overweight and his uniform took on the appearance of never being pressed. He wore neither decorations nor ribbons.

Smythe had been a lawyer before the war. He graduated from a nondescript university in Connecticut barely passing the bar exam. The fact that he was scarcely making a living in personal injury cases was more due to his lack of ambition than his talent.

When it became apparent that he was going to be drafted, he applied for a commission in the Navy's Judge Advocate General group. His application was accepted but almost immediately he was assigned to Navy Intelligence to work on Operation Overlord. Ultimately, he was cited for his work on the invasion and with French resistance forces. When the war ended, Smythe asked to stay in London where he felt comfortable and was assigned to the Embassy to handle cryptographic and courier services. With the Russians flexing their muscle on the continent, he was kept very busy.

"Parker's late," Foxworthy uttered through partially clenched teeth as he looked at his watch. He was definitely unhappy with the situation.

"I told him to come here directly from the airport," Smythe. explained. "Look, it was a simple retrieval assignment with an experienced operative. Heidi wouldn't let anything go wrong." Then he added, "You know Parker was our only choice."

Although Foxworthy had overall responsibility for the Navy at the Embassy, Smythe controlled intelligence operations. Both officers were well aware of their predicament. The untimely disappearance of their last courier was an embarrassment. With a hot war going on in Korea, the Far East had top resource priority. Their chance of getting another trained operative from Washington was slim at best. None of these circumstances alleviated their current responsibilities in Europe. The Russians saw the Korean conflict as the perfect time to mix things up in Europe. Neither one of them could afford to allow a breach of security at this point in their careers.

"You did at least review his security clearance," Foxworthy snapped as more of a statement than a question.

"There was a thorough background check to clear him for Top Secret. One of the comments even said he still wore his pea jacket from World War II. He's as clean as Jack Armstrong."

A rap at the door broke the tension. Penny Davenport entered with the morning mail.

"Good morning, Penelope."

"Good morning. Very little in the post today, sir. The priority teletypes are on top. There are a few more messages still being decrypted. You two look rather serious."

27

"We're just mulling the whereabouts of our new recruit. If he caught that early morning flight from Munich, he should have been opening the Embassy door this morning."

"I checked the manifest. He was on the flight. Maybe he had trouble getting a taxi. Do you need any more tea?"

Foxworthy shook his head. Smythe held up his cup.

"See if you can look up a scone."

"Penelope, check his hotel," Foxworthy said giving Smythe a glance of disgust. "See if you can track him down."

"Yes sir, I'll get right on it," she replied as she spun around. At the door she turned. "I think he's going to be just fine. Probably the traffic."

As the door closed, Captain Foxworthy looked directly at Smythe. "I can't believe that we got into a situation where we had to send an untrained simpleton on a sensitive mission."

"Look, I tend to agree with Penny. Parker's definitely naive, but not a simpleton.

He knows nothing about what's going on here and that's a definite advantage."

"We're putting a lot of……"

Foxworthy's words were stopped by the intercom buzzer. He pressed the button.

"Parker's on his way in," Penelope's voice cracked across the wires.

When the lieutenant stepped through the door wearing his navy dress blue uniform, he came to attention and saluted. The captain did not snap back

28

the usual "At ease." He wanted Parker to sweat for being late and obviously changing clothes.

Smythe broke the silence. "What the hell's the matter with you, Parker? I specifically told you to come directly here from the airport." Without waiting for a response he added, "Did you get the cigarettes?"

Parker casually reached into his inside coat pocket, slowly withdrew the pack of Camels and held it out in front of him. Although he appeared tense, he felt confident that the cigarettes were the important thing and some small diversion in routine would be quickly overlooked.

Smythe glowered as he rose and lumbered toward Parker, snatching the cigarettes. He squeezed the pack in several areas and nodded to Foxworthy.

"At ease, Parker. Did you have any problems?" Foxworthy asked.

"Not really, sir. I did get some catsup from my knockwurst on my civvies. I went back to the Wellington Arms to change so I could be presentable at the Embassy." Somehow, the lie came easily. Sensing it was time to shift to the offensive, he added, "Why didn't you tell me the contact was a woman? I nearly forgot my code words."

Now relaxing, Smythe slouched back in his seat. "We tell you as little as possible for your own good. Heidi is one of our best operatives." As he held the cigarettes he felt a twinge of satisfaction that his rookie got through his first assignment. "For today, Penelope will take you to the code room and you can help with some work that is piling up. We have you scheduled for a very routine delivery of crypto machine rotors to a destroyer doing some R and R in Bordeaux. Then you go on to Paris with some new code sheets for the Embassy. You'll be in uniform wearing a side arm."

"By the way, you're to turn your gun into Higgins at the end of each assignment. Is that clear?"

Parker didn't need to think. "Yes, sir."

"Dismissed." Foxworthy motioned toward the door.

When the door shut, Smythe tore open the cigarettes and withdrew a small cassette of microfilm and held it up to Foxworthy. Both men smiled.

CHAPTER FOUR

The Code Room was in the basement of the Embassy near its center. The imposing steel door was emblazoned with "Security Clearance Required." Penelope punched numbers into a small black box over the door handle "The code is changed daily," Penelope said swinging the door open. "I'll tell you later how to get the numbers. I don't think it affects the system to any great extent, but it should slow down any intruders," she added with a smile.

The room had no windows giving it a sterile appearance. A row of coding machines sat along the far wall. Four operators were typing at these stations. On the left wall were five Teletype machines, two of which were busy handling incoming messages while another had an operator sending an outgoing message. A row of small safes and locked files were on the right next to an embedded single large combination safe. The center of the room had a table for sorting, filing, and assigning work.

"Chad!" Penelope beckoned to a figure bent over the table.

"Hi," the figure responded looking up but not moving.

"Here's a new recruit who needs to keep busy for a day or two."

Chad stood up straight and turned from the table. "We could have used a little help earlier."

"Chad Conrad, I'd like you to meet Lt. James Parker," Penelope said. "Chad is an Embassy economic analyst."

He was taller than Parker by some four inches but probably weighed less. Tweed pants, a sweater, and an open collared shirt belied anything that would be tied to an accounting background. His open-faced smile was a pleasant surprise to Parker.

"Glad to meet you, Parker. From what I've heard we're lucky to have you on board," Chad smiled with the self-satisfaction of thinking up a Navy analogy. He waved Penelope off.

Chad gave Parker a quick tour around. "Most of the routine messages come in overnight. We are busy with these early on. There's usually a lull around our lunchtime, then the real rush begins about 2 PM when Washington wakes up. We've got a three-hour window when both of us are really up and running. The decoding is done on the standard step-rotor machines in which the rotor position sequences, left to right, and initial rotational settings are set to the code for the day. Pretty much the same as on board ship. No?"

"I think I can handle it," Parker nodded. He looked around. Mostly young people who probably looked at encoding and coding as the most boring part of their day. He guessed that little of real importance actually came over the Teletype since it passed through too many hands to be kept secret. Top Secret and For Your Eyes Only messages would be delivered by courier personnel.

"Only two of us set the rotors. All the rest just type," Chad added unnecessarily.

"What's an Economic Analyst doing in the coding room? You're not planning the economic coup of the British Empire, are you?"

"Parker, nobody at the embassy, except possibly the Ambassador, is who they say they are. I do all sorts of things, least of which is economic analysis. I've been here for two years. Not bad duty except for this damn coding room. The rest of the time I do some low level snooping around. Nothing very exciting, but the cocktail parties are usually a blast. They're a great way to meet a higher class of young ladies. What about you? Did you spend any time on the farm?"

"A destroyer in the Mediterranean is definitely not a farm."

Chad's brow furrowed. "You didn't go through training or orientation?"

"For what?" Parker asked slowly raising an eyebrow. "From what they've told me so far, I'm just a delivery boy."

Chad muffled a smirk. "Didn't they mention anything about the last two couriers?"

"They said they were 'lost', what the hell ever that means."

Chad tugged on Parker's coat sleeve and tilted his head. "I think we'd better have some coffee in the lunch room."

As a small boy Chad always wanted to be a policeman. His favorite game was cops and robbers and there was no doubt who was the cop. In elementary school he was always first to volunteer for crossing patrol so he could wear a large silver badge of authority. Upon graduation from high school, he wanted to apply for the Police Academy, but his parents would have none of it. "Go to college so you can get a good job. You'll starve as a Policeman," became almost an evening chant. Not the best of students, Chad thought about being a lawyer, but his grades weren't good enough. A high school counselor recommended study in Political Science and Chad had found his field. Getting his BA gave him an opportunity to apply for a position with the CIA and, after extensive interviewing, got accepted. His quick wit, charm, and sense of humor eventually got him posted to the station in the London Embassy where he was currently running a secretary at the Russian Embassy. Admittedly he was doing much better probing her in bed then probing for any secrets. Best of all, the Station Chief, Jack Evans, encouraged him to continue his efforts. For Chad this was a win-win situation.

The lunchroom was a small cafeteria for the lower echelon Embassy staff. The department heads and above, Chad explained, had their own private dining facilities. The cafeteria was nearly empty and the staff was busy preparing for the lunchtime rush. Chad filled a cup from the urn and handed it to Parker.

"This is one of the few places in England that you'll get a decent cup of coffee," Chad explained. "The coffee is free to pacify the expatriates. You can come here anytime during the day." They settled in on one of the tables. Chad leaned in toward Parker. "Look, I'm getting the idea you don't know what the hell is going on here at all. The only way couriers get 'lost' is by getting caught doing covert assignments then imprisoned or executed. Defecting usually for a large sum of money is another way of disappearing. The chance of just wandering down the wrong street is zero. Rumor here has it that one got caught and is being detained indefinitely. The other probably defected and is living in the lap of luxury in Brazil. So your assessment of delivery boy status is not correct at all."

James Parker's brow furrowed. Chad was probably right. They'd given him a gun to use without any specific instructions. He sipped his coffee. "Thanks for the input. For now I'm going to play delivery boy and see how long it lasts."

Chad was well into his coffee. "Well, if things get a bit hairy for you, feel free to come and talk things over with me. My assignments are very routine here but I am running a couple of Russians right now," Chad replied stretching the truth slightly. When's your next assignment?"

"Friday I take off to Bordeaux and then on to Paris with some codes and rotors."

"Well, I really don't think I'll need help in crypto today. Check in tomorrow morning. In the meantime I'll research the social events calendar and see if we can fit in a couple of smash cocktail parties to get you introduced around."

"Sounds like my kind of schedule," Parker smiled. He knew they were going to be great friends.

The next few days were a relaxing change of pace for Parker. Crypto duty in the morning, lunch with Conrad, then planning to see what cocktail party or other event they could squeeze out an invitation for or, if necessary, crash one. The sharply tailored look of a new uniform plus the staff braid sporting three rows of service ribbons always made a favorable impression. This was turning out to be a good assignment, and he would have a few wardroom stories to tell when he returned to the USS Perry.

Wednesday morning's message board brought him back to reality:

"Lt. Parker report in dress blues to Comdr. Smythe at 0900 Thursday."

"Penelope has booked you a 2 PM flight to Bordeaux to meet the USS Harris ETA 1700 wharfside at pier 14. This is your bag," Smythe said as he pointed to what looked like an ordinary canvas bag closed at the top with a steel cable.

Parker moved in for a better look.

"Kind of commonplace for secret documents," Parker noted.

"It's a relatively new procedure. As you know, we no longer use the hand cuff protocol. It turned out to be ineffective anyway."

Parker was glad to hear that.

"The cable has a lead seal," Smythe continued. "If the seal is broken or you lose your way somehow, the codes and rotors become 'compromised.' Those specific rotors and codes are then never used so no harm is done. However, I would advise you not to fuck up."

Parker nodded trying not to show any emotion.

"Deliver the bag to the Commanding Officer in the presence of the Communications Officer. The Captain will break the seal and remove the bag with the rotors. Get the two signatures on the receipt form in the bag.

They will immediately message us that the exchange has taken place. This will also let us know where you are."

"What about the stuff for Paris? Has that been called off?"

"No. The codes for next month are inside the bag, but in a black briefcase with a sealed cable through the top similar to the one here. At the embassy follow the same basic procedures as for the destroyer. The specific names for signing are in your orders for this delivery. The Embassy in Paris will message us also as soon as the delivery is complete."

Smythe paused, trying to discern if Parker was grasping everything.

"The whole courier procedure is quite simple. You will be following the same routine for each delivery. Occasionally they may give you something to return, but that would be rare. Do you speak French? You know the French don't warm up to foreigners."

"*Un pue de*," Parker replied. His French was worse than his German.

"I'd suggest you get a phrase book to read on the plane. By the way, don't leave the bags out of your sight at any time. Lose one of these and you'll be *numero uno* ass-hole around here."

"I'll do my best," Parker said. It sounded simple enough.

"All right. You'll be wearing a side arm. Use the diplomatic passport under your own name. Check out your gun from Higgins. Get some expense money, pick up your tickets from Penelope, and return here at 1100 for the bag. That should allow you plenty of time to get to Heathrow. You'll take the overnight train from

Bordeaux to Paris. And some good news….. you've got the weekend in Paris. Unless you have any questions, you are dismissed."

"Thank you, sir," Parker saluted and turned. *Thank you, I think.*

Smythe didn't bother to return the salute. That was just Mickey Mouse stuff. He had a job to do and he was doing it the best he could with what they had given him.

"How did the first mission go?" asked Higgins as he put a finish polish on the .45.

"OK," Parker replied. He was surprised that Higgins would even ask.

"Nothing special happen?"

"A piece of cake."

"Your gun was dirty. You should take better care of it. It could turn out be your best friend out there."

Parker was stunned. He never thought of cleaning the gun before he returned it.

"There was blood on the barrel," Higgins pointed out matter of factly.

"I….I cut myself. Some blood must have gotten on the gun somehow."

"It's not your blood type."

Parker was speechless. His eyes squinted.

Higgins paused long enough to study his reaction. "The report from the cleaners showed the same blood type on the pants. The station here is quite thorough, you know. We also have a record of every party you and Chad attended last week. When you fart, they make a recording of it."

Parker stared with disbelief then shook his head. "Well, I'll be damned."

"I get the feeling that you aren't taking this assignment very seriously. This is no Dick Tracy, Junior G-man escapade. You are out there alone on assignment and this can be a high stakes game. When you get back I want to spend some time with you on the range so you feel more comfortable with the gun. We can't afford to lose another courier."

"Th...thanks," Parker stuttered in reply. Maybe he had been taking things too lightly. Maybe that first assignment was successful by just pure luck. Higgins' concern seemed genuine. He also appreciated that he wasn't pressed for details about the blood.

"You'll be wearing this duty belt with your uniform. These deliveries are a lot less adventuresome than the ones where you are in civvies. You really only need to pay attention to what the hell you are doing. Where are the deliveries?"

"Bordeaux and Paris."

"How much expense money did you requisition?'

"I haven't yet. Probably a hundred."

"Look, let me give you another tip. Money is not an issue here. The mission is the issue. Take enough money. They really don't care as long as you turn in a decent expense account. Take some in francs, but most of it in dollars. Money can get you out of more trouble than that gun."

"Well, how much do you think I should take?"

"A thousand at the least," Higgins answered as he held the gun belt out to Parker.

"Sounds good to me," Parker replied as he fastened the belt. "And thanks for the advice. I'll bring you back something from Paris. Need anything?"

"Don't bother. I've been there and already got it. Wear a rubber. We need you back and in good health."

"See you in a couple of days."

Higgins nodded. A gun and money were OK, he thought, but dumb luck is what Parker really needed.

The flight schedule to Bordeaux was only about an hour. Parker passed through customs and immigration with a wave as he flashed the diplomatic passport. He was surprised how few people gave him a second look even with the duty belt, a .45 in its holster, and a canvas bag with a metal seal in plain view. He put his small suitcase in the overhead compartment, but kept the bag under the seat in front of him. By-passing the complementary cocktail, he put his foot on the bag as he dozed off.

In Bordeaux he was waiting on the pier when the USS Harris pulled smartly alongside and was the first to board.

"Permission to come aboard," was more a statement than a question.

"The captain is expecting you, sir. Report immediately to the wardroom," said the duty officer on deck. "Do you know the way?"

"I'm fresh off a can," Parker said as he turned forward.

Captain Morrison was sitting at the head of the wardroom table around which the department head officers were sitting. He was in the process of reviewing the duty roster and liberty schedules for the officers and men.

"Let's get the first and third watch off at 1830. Rotate the duty watch for the other two days. Give the men the standard liberty instructions. Liberty is up at 0600. This is a quiet port compared to some of the others so I expect them to get drunk, laid, and return without any trouble. If there is any, I'm holding the respective department heads responsible. The Plebes get liberty tomorrow at noon so they can get a city tour or something more sedate. Morely, stay here. The rest of you are dismissed."

The wardroom cleared. Captain Morrison extended his hand to Parker. "Welcome aboard. It's a surprise to see a line officer. Are you on TAD?"

"Yes, sir. I was on the Perry in the Med two weeks ago."

"Mmmm. That would be Commander Keiffer. We were in the same class at the Academy. Give him my regards."

"Yes, sir," Parker nodded making a mental note to not remember.

"OK, let's get the rotors and get you on your way."

Parker handed him the bag. Morrison broke the seal easily using two table knives as a wedge. The rotors were wrapped in a metal foil. He examined them and handed them to Morely who also looked them over.

"They look OK to me," Morely said while nodding.

Morrison looked directly at Parker. "You know, we didn't expect to be picking up rotors out here. We're on a "kiddy cruise" for Academy freshmen and doing the North Atlantic on our own. Things must be heating up here to be changing codes so quickly. What do you hear in London?"

"Really, nothing," Parker answered. He paused noting that Morrison's gaze did not change. "I'm just a messenger boy. They don't tell me a thing, sir."

Morrison had been out for three weeks on this cruise and felt uneasily out of touch. He wasn't going to give up so easily. He was desperate for news.

"Come on, now. There must be some scuttlebutt going around. You can't help but read the coded messages. What's going on?"

Parker could see where this was leading. "The messages are secret or top secret, sir, you know that. If you want my opinion, there's a lot of tension concerning what the Russians might do. Other than that they keep me pretty much in the dark."

"Shit, Parker. You're worthless. Next time bring me some goddamn news! Morely, get him a cab," Captain Morrison barked signing the receipt and shoving it towards Morely.

Parker's head nodded. The click clack of the train wheels was hypnotic. The lights in the compartment were on European dim as the night train for Paris made its way East. The train was definitely not an express, stopping what appeared to be every 15 minutes. He should talk with Penelope about this when he got back.

Suddenly the compartment door flew open snapping Parker out of his reverie. A boy about 12 followed by three younger girls and a woman who appeared to be their mother invaded the compartment. They were speaking French at a speed well beyond his comprehension. The boy unlatched the chains holding the overhead sleeping cots. The cots clattered down, the one over Parker bounced to rest inches from his head. The whole family began to change into their nightclothes in front of Parker without any inhibitions. He guessed the mother was in her early forties. Dropping all her clothes, she was facing him when their eyes met. He couldn't shift his eyes. The woman paused for a moment, turned away and finished changing into her nightgown.

Parker made himself comfortable on the lower seat, now his bed. He removed his gun belt and laid it between him and the wall. He took his shoes off and with the briefcase under his knees, drifted off to sleep hoping that he would shortly be awakened by a seductive kiss by his comely traveling companion.

The swaying of the train added to the deepness of Parker's sleep. The train stopped periodically at towns along the route beating out a now familiar rhythm. Parker's dream woman, strikingly like the Frenchwoman, was next to him. She was deftly unzipping his pants and began groping inside as the train lurched to a noisy stop. What she wanted was not in his pants. It was the black briefcase being slid out from beneath his knees.

Not fully awake, Parker rose up quickly striking his head on the cot above him with considerable force. Momentarily stunned he could only glimpse the compartment door opening and thief vanishing. He grabbed his gun. This time he knew where the safety was, snapping it off as he bolted towards the door. The corridor was dark, but he could hear the noise from a partially opened door towards the rear of the train.

Still not seeing anyone, he ran shoeless with the gun in his hand towards the sound. In the next car he could make out a figure in flight just at the other end.

"*Arrete!*" Parker blurted in one of the few French words he could remember. But the thief continued into the next car with Parker in hot pursuit.

A conductor partially blocked the narrow corridor, but the thief seemed to easily duck by him continuing towards the rear of the train. Parker was not closing the distance. He shouted out. "Stop, thief!" in hope that the conductor understood some English but the Frenchman did not seem to respond. Using an elbow to the solar plexus, he knocked him out of the way. The thief opened the door and wind and noise flooded the car. It was the last car of the train. The robber had reached the guardrail then turned as Parker approached.

It was the boy from the compartment.

"Give me the goddamn briefcase," Parker shouted over the clatter of the train waving his gun at the kid.

"He ees only a leetle boy," pleaded the conductor who was now close behind him.

Parker was close enough to see the terror in the boy's eyes. If he moved too fast, the kid could just drop the briefcase over the rail. That's all he needed. Secret codes scattered all over the damn French countryside.

He continued to stare at the boy and then cautiously put the gun on the floor. He slowly turned around towards the conductor taking out his wallet and deliberately counted off four $20 bills being sure the kid could see him. He handed him the money.

The conductor was stunned. Parker calmly said, "It's OK. It's OK," taking a guess that the Frenchman would understand. He then turned towards the kid and repeated his count off of four more $20 bills. The kid understood, immediately offering the briefcase in exchange for the money.

Parker gave a sigh of relief as he grabbed the briefcase. He picked up the gun and placed it in his waistband. Higgins was right again.

With the $80 in hand, the kid marched towards their compartment with Parker nearly in lock step. As they approached the door, Parker snatched the money from the kid's hand and gave him a boot through the door with his foot. He gathered his things and spent the rest of the night in the club car.

CHAPTER FIVE

Parker's first view of Paris was by taxi. He was able to spot the Eiffel Tower and identify the Champs-Elysees remembered from his high school geography class. After speeding down a few broad thoroughfares, the taxi made its way more slowly through many small streets before it arrived at the American embassy. Parker could see that he was getting "the tour", but he didn't care. It wasn't his money. Besides, it gave him a chance to relax.

It was a beautiful day to be in Paris, he thought, but he couldn't seem to shake the events of the last night. The significance of nearly losing the diplomatic pouch on the train was just starting to sink in. He certainly wasn't planning on making the Navy a career, but a clean service record was important to him. It was more a question of personal pride than patriotism. Had he lost the briefcase, the episode would forever be on his service record labeling him as a goof up. A squealing of the taxi brakes and an abrupt stop snapped Parker out his reverie.

The American Embassy in Paris was large, but not imposing. A black metal seven-foot tall fence and the American flag were dead giveaways. Inside the gates, the cobblestone driveway added charm. Surprisingly, no activity was evident.

"I'm Geoffrey Simmons," said a young, slightly built man in the receiving hall. He explained that he was an Undersecretary at the Embassy. "I'm one of the persons who will be signing for the codes. The other fellow will be down in a minute." He led Parker into one of the meeting rooms. The room was meticulously decorated and made the London seem stodgy by comparison "You can check your manifest."

Parker found the name on his orders. "I'll need your identification papers before I can release the briefcase. By the way, where is everyone? Other than you and the Marine guard, there's no one around. Is this a holiday or something?"

"It's Friday afternoon and just about everyone has checked out for the weekend," Simmons answered. He took a thin wallet from his inside coat pocket and laid his photo identification cards on the table in front of Parker. "Incidentally, I was instructed to tell you that you're the Senior Officer Present in the Paris district till 0800 Monday morning."

"What do you mean, Senior Officer Present," Parker said with surprise. "A Lieutenant, junior grade, doesn't sound very senior to me."

"All the captains, colonels, and commanders checked themselves out. They knew you were coming. You are not only the SOP, but the only United States Military Officer of record on duty in Paris."

"Just what the hell does that mean?"

"Really, not much. We're virtually closed up here. Standard procedure requires that you check in with the Central Police Station. You're expected to arrive prior to 1800. They will want to keep in touch with you all weekend in case of any trouble with U.S. military personnel on leave. We've got you booked into Hotel D'Anna right off the Etoile and close to the Station. It's modest, but you'll find it quite suitable. Check back with us Monday morning just before your flight to London in case we have anything to send back."

The second man arrived and Parker checked his credentials, which also matched the manifest.

"I'll get you a taxi to take you to the Police Station," Simmons said as he took possession of the briefcase.

"Thanks. I didn't expect to be working over the weekend."

"Look at it as a work experience."

When the taxi arrived, Parker removed his gun belt and stuffed it into his overnight bag. His eyes immediately closed as he leaned back in his seat. He had hardly slept at all on the train. His mind drifted. He had almost killed that kid. He had the safety off. He had to be more careful. He…….

* * *

Boris Chernoff bent over the morning mail. His office was a dimly lighted cubicle on the fourth floor of the KGB headquarters in East Berlin. A simple decoded message from his contact in London caught his eye. "New London courier. Parker. Code drop. Paris. Friday. No photos or background available."

Chernoff hated Fridays. Everything seemed to focus on the weekend, screwing up any chance of a quiet Saturday or Sunday in the country. He also hated his office. He resented how rapidly Western Europe was recovering from the war and it bothered him that the Russian block was making virtually no progress. The lighting was terrible. He rose from the desk and walked towards the window with a noticeable limp.

He turned and shouted, "Ivan, get in here!"

The limp bothered him, but it was a small price to pay to help get rid of Hitler. Early in 1942 he found himself defending against the German invasion as a Private in the Army. It was utter confusion as the Germans overran the frontier. Chenoff's private joke was that he was wounded in the leg from the backside as he was attacking the Germans. During his hospital recuperation he served as an interpreter for the medical staff since he spoke several Russian dialects as well as Polish and German. Languages came easy for him. Several of the field doctors had trained in England, so he readily picked up English as well. After his release from the hospital, the army found that his knowledge of German and English was of much better use to them than his skill with a rifle. Besides, the wound would never fully heal.

The leg prevented him from getting the exercise he really needed. His parents were both large people and inactivity put on pounds easily. Luckily, his own discipline in exercising his upper body kept his weight in control although at the top limit on the charts. For 45 years old he considered himself in good physical condition. His leg bothered him when it was cold and the office was always cold in the mornings. The heat was turned off in April and wouldn't be turned on till November.

"Ivan!" he shouted in almost a scream.

The door burst open. The crinkled uniform housed a young man holding a note pad.

"Good morning, Comrade."

"Don't give me that Comrade crap. Get in here when I call, not ten minutes later!"

"I was on the phone with…."

"Then you put the phone down when I call," Chernoff said emphatically with clenched teeth. "Get this message to our contact in Paris right now." He scrawled four words vertically on a memo pad and handed it to Ivan. Antoine was one of his most reliable men in the field. He'd have all the information he'd need on this by Monday. He'd already helped neutralize two couriers. Chernoff didn't want the London Intelligence network feeling at ease if he could help it.

Ivan returned to his desk. The message to Paris was nonsense.

Pigeon
Station
Roosts
Roots

He sent it knowing the instructions would be understood on the other end.

* * *

"So, you are *le gros fromage* for the weekend," chief of police Marceau said with a half smile as he looked at the young officer. "Your responsibilities are simple. Everything must be kept quiet and under control. We will give you a car and two gendarmes to escort you. You will mainly patrol the Montmartre district where the prostitutes work. Individual managers control most of them. You call them pimps, no? There are only two whorehouses in the area. Be sure to check them out. We expect you to see that Americans in uniform behave themselves."

Marceau paused for some indication of acknowledgment. Parker nodded, still drowsy from his lack of sleep.

"No need to check in until 0800 Monday. I will be available if you need any help, *mon ami.*"

"*Oui*," answered Parker with the only French he could muster.

Parker found the car and the two escorts. Unfortunately, they spoke almost no English so most of the communications were by hand signals or grunts. Parker tossed his handbag into the rear seat. The car accelerated down the Champs at remarkable speed with the blue light flashing for no apparent reason. The driver was laughing as pedestrians scurried out of the way.

The streets of the Montmartre area were just beginning to be filled with the nocturnal wanderers. The tourists, natives, and prostitutes were easily identified. Only an occasional American serviceman was sighted rapidly making arrangements, which seemed to be quite amicable. Somewhat bored, but mainly tired, Parker made a gesture as if he were holding a coffee mug and brought it to his lips. Both escorts nodded understandingly and the car took off again with lights flashing making two right turns, stopping under an international no-parking symbol. They motioned Parker to follow as they entered the building and walked up the stairs. It didn't look like a café and it wasn't.

A heavy set woman in fine attire and fashionably coiffured hair opened the door to a large, lavishly

51

7furnished seating room and motioned for them to enter. She looked at Parker.

"You must be ……"

"Ze *gros fromage,*" Parker interrupted.

She smiled.

"I'm Marie, the manager," she said in nearly perfect English. "I have just what you want, Commander."

"Look, I'm just a Lieutenant. What I really need is a cup of coffee."

"Sit down here. I'll be right back."

Parker's escorts were grinning. They motioned to the effect that they were going back down and they would wait for him in the car. It was surprising how well they were getting along without saying a word. Parker sank into a red velvet couch that nearly consumed him. He gazed at the ceiling from which a huge dazzling crystal chandelier hung. This was no coffee shop.

Marie returned and handed Parker a steaming cup. "I put just a touch of cognac to take the bitterness out. I've sent for Madeline. She will take charge. Don't worry, there is no cost for you."

Before Parker could reply, a smallish figure entered the room dressed in a silk robe tied loosely. She was barefooted. She moved gracefully, took Parker by his empty hand and silently led him out and down the hall and into a dimly lit room. There was a lone bed set directly in the center. Large paintings of naked women in erotic poses graced the walls. Madeline pulled Parker alongside her on the bed, loosened her robe and turned to kiss him.

He slowly placed the coffee cup down on the floor.

Sex came pleasantly that night, without tension or pressure. Madeline quickly put Parker at ease showing a dimension of experience far beyond that of Parker's mid-west Ohio upbringing. Until the seventh grade he had not really taken much notice of the opposite sex. It was only when he was invited to his first boy-girl party that his age of sexual experimentation began. He got matched up with a young girl who was a light year ahead of him, but fortunately he was a quick study and caught up with her after a few dates. But, because of his limited experience, there was always some apprehension that he wasn't doing things the best way. This night, Madeline led him through a sequence of sexual vignettes with a gentle touch of an expert guide.

The night passed quickly. Madeline sat at the dressing table brushing her hair as the morning sunlight began entering the room. She heard Parker stir. She turned and walked slowly towards him, her kimono untied.

"Jimmy, you like Madeline, no?"

Parker was barely awake, but nodded his head sensing she wanted his confirmation.

"I don't belong here," she pouted. "They brought me here as a little girl. They taught me all those bad things. I don't know anything else. I need to get away, but they keep me here like a prisoner. If I just had enough money, I could get out of here, go back to school, and make something of myself," her eyes welling with tears.

Parker took his first real look at the girl. Her slight build gave the appearance of youth. He could see no lines at the corner of her eyes yet he knew from her performance that she was not a beginner.

"Jimmy, you help me," she pleaded as she bent down over the bed to kiss him.

Parker sat up and twisted to dodge the kiss. "There's nothing I can do to help you. I'm on duty here for just a day or two and then I'm back to London." If Madeline was leading Parker on a guilt trip, it was beginning to work. He started to feel uneasy and it was time to get out of there. He gently brushed her hair aside and gave her an avuncular kiss, pushing her slowly away. He spied his trousers on the floor, and started to get out of bed.

She grabbed his shoulders and pushed him back down.

"Five hundred American dollars will take me out of here and give me a new life," she pleaded in remarkably improved English.

Parker gently shrugged off her grip and moved her aside on the bed. "I should check in with the Chief of Police," he said trying to change the subject. He snatched his pants on his way to the bathroom. He looked into the mirror. The face staring back had a one-day stubble. He leaned forward to take a better look. *What's a kid from Cleveland doing in a Parisian whorehouse?* He shrugged his shoulders and splashed some water on his face sweeping him back to reality. Stepping into his trousers, he quickly checked his wallet. The money was all there. Maybe Madeline was telling the truth. Maybe all she needed was a fresh start. He opened the door into the bedroom. Madeline was still on the bed, sobbing.

"I'll see what I can do," he said. "Now take me downstairs."

In the lounge, Marie sat reading the morning newspaper. She looked up when Parker and Madeline entered. "*Bon jour*, commander."

"*Bon jour*, Marie," Parker responded accepting the promotion. He gave Madeline a parting peck on the cheek, turned her around, and pushed her back through the door and closed it.

"I want to thank you for your hospitality," Parker said politely.

"The pleasure was ours. We felt very secure to know that the chief of American military forces was relaxing in our humble abode. Was everything satisfactory?"

"Yes, but I want to talk to you about Madeline. She feels that she is virtually a ..."

"Prisoner," Marie finished his sentence. "They all say that. Let me tell you, captain, that the supply of women far exceeds the demand in this part of France. Our employees are free to come and go as they please."

"But..."

Marie cut him off with a wag of her index finger. "She asked you for money, didn't she?"

Parker's pause signaled agreement.

"They all do. They won't rob you. It's easier for them to talk you out of it. Commander, go down to your car and talk to your guards and see what they think. You all will have a good laugh. *Au revoir, capitaine.*"

Parker made his way down slowly. He had half a notion to get his gun out of his bag and rescue the girl. After all, he was the Supreme Commander of the American Forces, or something like that. On second thought, it seemed like a dumb idea.

The guards were sleeping in the car. Parker banged the side. They jumped out and began chattering in French. He made several gestures waving his hands outlining the female form. He smiled, they smiled. He tried to get the idea across that Madeline was being held prisoner by putting his wrists together and pretended to wind them with a chord. They roared with laughter. The correct message was not coming across. He gave up. He laughed too.

* * *

"Here's a message just brought in from Paris," Ivan said as he handed a small envelope to Boris.

Boris tore the envelope open. It was a small thank you card. He opened up to the blank side, placed it over the lamp on his desk and waited.

He thought the whole process was stupid. He knew that both radio and telephone transmissions from Paris were monitored, but this method by mail took four days. He would have preferred to use clear language over a telephone and let the Americans try to figure out what he was talking about, but his superiors would have had his hide. Americans were rumored to have a laser communication device in the testing stage to transmit messages over short ranges with total security but he hadn't seen anything of it as yet. In the mean time both sides had to put up with couriers or other routine conveyances.

The message slowly appeared "P made routine code delivery to embassy. Spent night in Madam Marie's. Did tourist things. No contacts. Departed Monday. Seems harmless. A."

"Thanks for nothing, Antoine," Boris muttered.

"What did you say, Comrade?"

"Nothing," Boris replied as he continued to mutter.

He turned to Ivan, "Tell our London office to inform us as soon as this new courier, Parker, goes on his next trip. See if they can dig up some details on his background. We need a photo at least. Sooner or later he's going to make a drop or retrieval and I want to know about it."

Ivan started to leave, then turned back toward Chernoff.

"I'm on duty this weekend, and I need cigarettes. I just can't seem to shake the habit. If you're planning to go to West Berlin this weekend, I'd appreciate some American packs.

He grabbed in his pocket and pulled a fist full of American dollar bills.

Boris might have been tempted by the dollars for an instant, but was much too wily. He knew that the room was bugged. He was indeed going to spend part of the weekend in West Berlin where he could at least get a decent meal. He resented the prosperity of the West but did not hesitate to take advantage of it when he could.

"You should try harder to quit. It's a filthy habit. I heard some Turkish cigarettes are coming in over the weekend. Put your order in for them," Chernoff smirked. He knew that Ivan was just following orders to test him, but he was growing tired of these cheap tricks.

Ivan pocketed the money and left.

Boris sank back into his seat pondering Parker. He relished the current situation. He had managed to take two couriers out of action from the London CIA branch within weeks of each other. He could only imagine how panicky Evans must have been. He had never met his London counterpart; in fact he'd never been to London, but thought of him as a long distance chess opponent only using agents and couriers as pawns.

Their strategy on Parker would be simple. Let him get confident with a few uninterrupted missions, then put the pressure on. He must have a weakness. The others did and they would find it. It troubled him that there was no background data on Parker. But he wasn't worried. He'd get to him when the time was right.

Boris got up and went to the radiator. His leg was stiff. He looked out the window. The fog from his breath steamed the window and for an instant he saw the faces of his wife and children that he lost years ago. Damn Germans! He hated them and it was ironic that he was now living in the center of Germany. He wanted revenge for the loss of his family during the war, but there was no revenge to be had. Germany was beaten and would stay beaten in the East. His work was elsewhere.

He shook his head to clear the memories. He resolved to have a second glass of wine after dinner tonight.

CHAPTER SIX

Parker passed the small box across the desk to Penelope. "Just a little gift from Paris for all the help you've been"

"That's very kind of you, James," Penelope smiled and began to unwrap the Chanel Number 5. "This is wonderful but there are very few occasions now where I could wear such an expensive perfume."

"Just put some in the bath water tonight and see if it carries over till tomorrow."

"Now, James."

"I'll just breeze in tomorrow early and see if you've attracted a crowd of eager young male attaches."

"You may not get a chance. I've got your schedule for the coming week. You're going to be frightfully busy."

"Damn it. I might need some help then. My mother's birthday is coming up soon and I'd like to get her a cashmere sweater that I've heard so much about. You got any tips where I can get something like that?"

"Selfridges is only a short distance away from the Embassy and on my way home. Call in when you finish debriefing. If we leave early we can visit their export shop before it closes."

"Sounds good to me. I'm sure Mom will be pleased."

Parker's briefing with Commander Smythe confirmed Penelope's prediction. "You will leave

Monday morning in uniform and deliver packets to certain NATO capitals," Smythe began in a monotone. "We've arranged for some commercial transportation to cover the route in the quickest time. You will be gone for about a week, so take a couple of changes of clothes. The items you will be carrying are highly classified. See Higgins at 1100 for additional pistol practice. He says you stink. Penelope will arrange transportation and process your cash advance request. Report at 0900 Monday to pick up a diplomatic pouch. It will contain sealed packets marked for the respective embassies. Be super careful. The contents are very sensitive. Evans from CIA wants to see you next for a few minutes. His office is on the second floor."

Parker got up and thought it proper to give a salute before departing.

Smythe gave a quick wave as a substitute for a return salute. "Good Luck."

Evans rose to greet Parker with a handshake. "Sit down, lieutenant. It's time we got to know each other a little better."

On first glance there was nothing mysterious about Evans' appearance. Less than average height, he exhibited a Napoleonic edge, which was immediately evident. His speech pattern was rapid and his eyes seemed to be trying to penetrate your soul to see if you had something to hide. His title at the Embassy was Administrative Assistant, but it was open knowledge he was the CIA Station Chief in London. Rumor had it that he was under an edict to redefine the Russian threat to NATO now that the Korean situation appeared to be at a stalemate. The Company was putting pressure on the station for results but not willing to commit additional resources. Normally Evans was high strung, but this morning he looked simply nervous.

"Foxworthy says you have performed well on your courier assignments," Evans stated in clipped words.

Parker tilted his head and nodded agreement. Their first meeting since a passing introduction at one of the Embassy affairs. He felt no need to say anything at this point.

"Next week's assignment is basically a NATO assignment. The packets you will be delivering contain the missing parts of previous transmissions detailing NATO's plan to counter a surprise strike by the Russians. On the face of it, the papers appear quite innocuous, but when linked to previously transmitted documents they will complete our order of battle. Obviously we need you to be particularly on guard."

Evans' eyes did not shift as he continued.

"We've had some trouble with couriers as you know. My guess is that you have been already spotted and may be shadowed from time to time. Our plan is to make this run seem like a routine Embassy drop by mixing military transportation with some commercial flights. You will be picking up some meaningless documents and we want you to appear casual. Do some tourist things. But we want you to be alert and try to spot anyone who looks suspicious. Make a mental note of their description and we'll run it through our files to see if there is a match."

"I'll do my best," Parker replied.

"It's not just your best we're looking for. I'm talking with you to make sure you take your assignments very seriously. We just didn't lose two couriers, something happened to them. I'm not known for being subtle. We only know that they did not come back from their assignments and their packages were compromised."

Evans leaned forward, both forearms on the desk with clenched fists to be sure he had Parker's attention.

"The Embassy is on an alert status. If the Russians suspect your mission is anything other than routine, they will do what they need to obtain the information or, at the least, interrupt our lines of communications. You are definitely at risk and we want you to understand that."

Parker's eyes widened. He suddenly felt uncomfortable. His back on the leather chair felt damp.

"Whatever happened to Foxworthy's policy of telling me as little as possible?"

"We still think that is the best policy. The Russians won't move on you unless they think you know something or have something important that they want. However, we are desperately short handed and may need to temporarily expand your role here."

"Just what does that mean?"

"Let's get this delivery out of the way first. I want you to be sure you don't blab anything about your assignments. We think there might be a mole at the Embassy."

"A mole."

"It's a double agent, Parker. A double agent."

"A double agent," Parker repeated. He was beginning to sound like an echo.

The telephone rang.

"Oh, by the way, be sure to see Higgins this morning," Evans said as he rose signaling the end of the meeting. "He says you still need some target practice."

Parker rose, expecting a handshake, but Evans simply picked up the phone turning in his chair towards the back wall. Parker bit his lip reminding himself to talk to Higgins about the consequences of blabbing.

The phone call was prearranged with his secretary to break off the meeting. Evans really didn't give a rat's ass about the NATO plans; that was the Embassy's worry. He was trying to size Parker up in case they had to use him for other things. He placed the phone on the receiver and bent over the desk. On a small pad he wrote the initial P and added a question mark. He'd decide later.

It was 1105 when Parker caught up with Higgins at the practice range. The range was the bomb shelter built in early 1940 when the German air raids were just starting. This lower level housed several off-limit areas that Parker was not really anxious to learn about.

"How did you like Paris?" asked Higgins with a grin.

"Great. I met an old friend of yours at Madam Marie's. Annette. I didn't know you made it that far inland."

"I had a Shore Patrol assignment to transport an AWOL to the Independence at Cannes two years ago. Did you bring anything back?"

"Just an itch here," Parker answered pointing to the palm of his right hand. "Look, Chief, I know I'm a lousy shot but I'd appreciate it if you'd keep my level of expertise a private matter."

"I only report the truth."

"Well, I don't. Any more comments on my marksmanship and I let it slip that your Parisian friend said that you had the smallest dick she'd seen since she had sex with a munchkin. Now let's get started."

Higgins reluctantly absorbed the message and handed Parker the ear protectors.

"Here's your .45 all cleaned up. Let's see your technique on firing a full clip. I won't interrupt."

Parker grabbed the pistol, aimed, and pulled the trigger. Nothing happened. Sheepishly he took the safety off and pulled the trigger. Nothing happened. With a jerk he pulled the slide back placing a shell in the chamber and proceeded to fire the next six shots off in the direction of the target with a staccato tempo.

Chief Higgins turned away desperately trying to suppress a grin. Quickly gaining control, he turned around and pulled the target closer for Parker to see.

"You sure aren't wearing out the target," Higgins taunted as the virgin card appeared.

"Look, we'll try a two handed approach. Line up the gun and squeeze the trigger. You're letting it pull your hand back throwing the line way off. There's a lot of kick in a .45. Use two hands and let the gun go upward while still keeping your line. Lower it back to the target and fire again. Don't rush it, but don't waste any time. Do it methodically."

The Chief demonstrated with the gun without firing, then reloaded a clip.

Parker clenched his teeth as he drew a bead on the target and squeezed. The target fluttered. A shot of adrenaline sped through his veins. He lowered the gun, then squeezed again. A miss. Another miss. Another miss. Then a vision of Higgins laughing popped into Parker's head and the target quivered twice more.

Higgins drew the target in with some sense of pride.

"You're making some progress," Higgins said putting his finger through one of the holes.

"Thanks. I think it's time for lunch."

Chad Conrad grabbed Parker as soon as he entered the cafeteria.

"How did you do in France?"

"Great, except I nearly killed a kid on the train. The brat snatched my case and I came this close to drilling him. I've got to get my act together a little better," Parker replied as he grabbed a tray.

Funny, Parker thought, I don't remember telling him I had a Paris assignment.

"What are you up to? Anything new on that dame at the Russian embassy?" Parker queried trying to change the subject.

"I'm doing OK, but I'm taking it slow. She has some sensitive areas I have to explore. Want to see if she has a friend?"

"It looks as if I'm going to be very busy next week, but keep me in mind"

"Anything exciting?"

"Can't say," Parker shot back taking a ham sandwich.

"They told me to keep my mouth shut. Something about a raccoon or chipmunk," as Parker made a stab at some humor which Chad ignored.

"What do you know about your boss, Evans?" Parker asked.

"He's a tight ass. Doesn't like me too much. Thinks I'm too laid back. But that's just my style. I still deliver when he needs it so he really can't bitch. We're short handed which makes everyone edgy. Why do you ask?"

"Just trying to make conversation," Parker lied.

Chad led the way towards the empty seats next to the two best looking female clerks at the Embassy.

"Alice and Betty, this is Lieutenant Parker. Mind if we join you?" Chad put forth his full barrage of charm.

They motioned for them to sit.

At 1530 Parker entered Penelope's office.

"Just thought I'd take you up on that shopping trip. Coding is very slow today and I'm just marking time."

"Foxworthy and Smythe are both out of the office this afternoon and I'm due for some free time. I've got some things I want to look at in Selfridges. It's just two blocks away. Let me lock up a few things and we'll be off."

Outside on the Selfridges marquee was a large statue of newly crowned Queen Elizabeth on horseback in celebration of the coronation. Inside, the store was crowded. England was just getting off its wartime economy and there was a pent-up demand for everything. Penelope went to see about some woman's clothing items and Parker tagged along just taking in the sights. He kept busy by converting prices from pounds to dollars.

"Quite expensive," Parker commented as Penelope held up a pair of slacks.

"Our way of paying for the war, I guess," she replied as she continued eyeing the slacks. "We can't wear trousers at the embassy, but this will be great for the weekend or on holiday. After I ring these up, we'll head for the export shop and look for that sweater for Mum."

The Export Shop was on the seventh floor. It was cordoned off from the main shopping areas. An elderly gentleman sat in a chair partially blocking their way. He looked up at Parker and waved him through.

"They normally ask for passports, but the uniform is all that's necessary. If you have to, tell them I'm your wife."

Parker raised an eyebrow. Penelope led him along through the racks of fashionable clothing items, noticeably a step up from the more prosaic displays on the lower floors.

"The cashmere sweaters are over this way. They're not any in the main store.

They 're too expensive for the British, but you can get them for half the regular retail price because we need the dollars."

Penelope led the way to a stack of cashmere sweaters of different colors.

"Is this one suitable, lieutenant? Do you like pink?" Penelope teased as she held the sweater to her front letting it follow her form. The pink accented her dark hair and added to the blush of her cheeks.

"Mother never looked like that," Parker replied picking up the cue. "See if they have one a size larger and I'll take it." He moved towards Penelope and ran his hand over the garment pressing it against her body.

"I never felt anything so soft and smooth." He stared directly into her eyes. She did not retreat.

"They won't allow you take it with you," she said breaking the spell. "You'll have to send it. They'll make the arrangements including the duty when you pay the bill."

The pair exited onto Oxford Street.

"You should let me buy you dinner for all your help. I'd have to spend a week in that store before I could find my way around. Mom will be very pleased," Parker added as he held her hand as they crossed the street.

"That's a good idea. We can walk to my flat. I need to change out of these working clothes. You're fine. You'll be accepted anywhere in that uniform. By the way, the embassy tailor made a good job on those new dress blues. Did you really earn all those ribbons?"

"All but one. Smythe felt that I needed a sixth ribbon for symmetry. He took it upon himself to award me a good conduct medal for my enlisted time between the wars. It's a secret."

"You can trust me," Penelope said as they climbed the stairs to the third floor of a brownstone building.

Her flat looked Spartan. The furniture was simple with no flair in color. It was dark and cold. Parker could never get used to the lack of central heating or the dimly lighted rooms that Europeans took for granted.

Penelope lit a gas heater in the sitting room. James came over to warm his hands.

"The chill will be off the room in a moment," Penelope assured. "Relax for awhile." She reached over toward Parker loosened his tie and unbuttoned his collar button. "That looks better."

As she started to turn away Parker grabbed her arm and stopped her.

"I'm relaxing. How about you?" Parker said. Slowly he undid the top button on her blouse.

Penelope raised her head and looked into Parker's eyes. "Tell me something about yourself, James. What were you like as a boy? Do you have any brothers or sisters? What do you really think of the British?" Another button on Parker's shirt came undone.

"Quiet, one sister, and very nice people, especially you." Parker replied as another button on her blouse came undone. "You're a mystery woman around the embassy. No one talks about you. I don't know if that's good or bad."

"The least said, the better. I'm very efficient and I'm good at whatever I'm told to do." She unfastened another button. "What more could anyone ask?"

Slowly, button by button, they proceeded as if they were performing some ancient mating ritual. Parker felt the room heating up. Their bodies were not touching, but their hands were busy.

Penelope's blouse dropped to the floor. Her breasts were small but firm showing that she really didn't need the bra that he had unsnapped.

"How about you? What were you like as a girl? Do you have any brothers or sisters? How long have you been working at the embassy?" Parker mocked. He reached around to her back and found the zipper on her skirt.

"Noisy, an only child, and about three years," Penelope said matching Parker's cadence. Her skirt dropped. She unbuckled his belt.

The room was warm now. The game continued towards the bedroom leaving a trail of clothing. She countered every one of Parker's moves and quips.

There was no dinner that evening.

The room was cold when Parker awoke. Penelope was already in the kitchen and had the teapot steaming. Her eyes were red from crying. Trying to put on a good face, she turned towards Parker and smiled.

"I'd offer you breakfast, but I'm not a very good cook."

James seated himself at a small table in the kitchen. He was famished. Remarkably, the tea was good and he returned her smile.

"Look, James. We really shouldn't have done this. I need to tell you not to expect a relationship." She placed her fingers over his lips before he could reply, "I like you very much but the timing is all wrong. Besides I'm at least ten years older than you."

"You mean the sex was too adolescent?"

"No, on the contrary, it was good. It just isn't the right time. You'll have finished your assignment and returned to your ship before we could even get to know each other."

"Well, at least I know where I stand. I felt we had something good started."

"That's just the point. I don't want it to start. What no one wants to tell you is that I married an American from the Embassy about five years ago. At that time he was just beginning his career and we were very much in love. He began to have mission assignments on the continent and one day he just didn't come back. There was no explanation from the Embassy. He just disappeared. Out of guilt, they offered me a job to tide me over. The work was good for me and it keeps me occupied, but the thought of another loss haunts me."

"I'm sorry, Penelope," Parker said with sincerity. He had never lost a close relative, but could imagine how devastated he would be if his mother had suddenly passed away.

"Let's get going. I'll lock up here and give you a half-hour head start. You don't want to be late."

CHAPTER SEVEN

The call to report to Smythe's office came to the code room around 1100.

"Parker, we've got a few changes in your trip next week. Dress Blues all the way except at the end where we want you to take two days R and R in Copenhagen wearing civilian clothes. Relax and get to know the Danes. Do all the tourist stuff and it's important to get to know the center of town well. You'll be working there on some assignments in the near future. Any questions?"

"No," Parker answered shrugging his shoulders. He really didn't know what questions to ask.

"OK. Here's your schedule," Smythe said as he handed Parker the single page. "Paris, again, Rome, Bonn, Amsterdam, Brussels, Copenhagen. You'll use a diplomatic pouch. A sealed envelope inside is labeled for each embassy. The embassies will reseal the pouch and include some trivial, unclassified material just for show. The embassies will arrange for overnight lodging except for Copenhagen where we will make your reservations. Choose something upscale. Penelope will help you. You will go military from here to Paris and to Rome. The rest of the route will be commercial. We're trying to make this run appear as casual as possible."

Parker nodded studying the itinerary. "Any Senior Officer Present crap?"

"Your overnight stay in Amsterdam may be a little dicey. We have no official military presence there so you will be automatically SOP. It's a popular military leave town. We have issued orders to the Danish Embassy that you are to be strictly off duty in Copenhagen."

Parker raised an eyebrow as he surveyed the schedule. What was not on the list was interesting. NATO had ten members on the continent. Evidently some were not going to get the word. Luxembourg was too small to be concerned about. Norway was probably safe in the initial days of an attack, so what the hell. Portugal was not in the line of battle. It looked like the recent joiners, Turkey and Greece, would be sacrificial lambs. Bonn must be just a courtesy stop.

"Remember, try to act as casual as you can without getting sloppy. If you get the SOP *crap* in Amsterdam, keep the pouch at the embassy for security. Same thing when you are looking around Copenhagen."

Parker noted the emphasis he placed on crap and nodded his acquiescence.

"Oh, another thing. Take along an extra $500 or so. You are to do some tourist type shopping at each stop, even if you have to do it in the airport. Keep the receipts. Buy gifts that you can easily pack in your luggage."

"That's going to be different."

"Parker," Smythe said as he leaned forward on his desk. "Stay alert. This is important work you are doing. We don't want anything to go wrong."

Neither do I, Parker thought.

"You will be leaving Monday as scheduled."

"All right, here's the plan for the weekend." Chad was beaming. "There's a reception at the French

Embassy on Friday to introduce a new envoy. The French always do it up right. Lots of food, champagne and great looking women. It will be a blast. You don't want to miss this one, James. On Saturday I've got you fixed up with Betty for something more casual….."

"I'm not really in the mood for a lot of partying, Chad," Parker interrupted. It was difficult for him to come down to the realization that the perfect night with Penelope was just a one-time thing. In their brief conversations over the past two days, there wasn't the slightest clue on her part that something had happened between them. He realized it was over, but he was reluctant to accept that, in Penelope's mind, it might not have even started. "Besides, Higgins told me that the Embassy monitors everything we do," he added.

"Fuck Higgins. That old fart can't remember when he was young. Look, if something is bothering you, there's nothing like an embassy gig to lift you up. There are a lot of people you should be meeting. Besides, Alice won't date if you don't double with Betty. You're not going to let a buddy down, are you?"

"You can talk Alice out of her nylons without any help from me."

"Alice said it in clear language. It's double or nothing."

There was a definite pause. Chad was a tough act to turn down.

"OK, I'll sign on, but nothing on Sunday. I've got some work to do Monday."

"You won't regret it, James. Now here's the scoop on Betty," Chad put his hand on Parker's shoulder as they walked towards the coding room.

The Embassy Limo was shuttling the American guests to the French Embassy. This way each guest took on the same level of importance as well as solving the parking problem.

The main ballroom was extravagantly ornate graced with finely chiseled crystal chandeliers. Large mirrored walls exaggerated the size of the room, which contained over one hundred dignitaries. A string trio was softly filling in background music. Conrad was busy introducing Parker around and had developed a code to tag the really important ones. He took particular care with the Russian entourage.

"Vice Chairman Gorkin, this is Lieutenant Parker. He is new at the Embassy," Chad said. Gorkin had arrived earlier and was finding that the champagne insidious compared to the vodka. They shook hands and Parker was impressed with the strength of his grip.

"I was in Russian Navy. We might find much to talk about, Lieutenant."

"I am sure I would disappoint you. My career has been quite uneventful."

"Well, there will be no battles here tonight. Tonight we are comrades with champagne, no?" Gorkin asked as he released his grip.

Parker was glad to be led toward a tall, slender young woman dressed all in black.

Chad and the woman exchanged knowing glances.

"James, this is Catherine, one of the officials at the Russian embassy." Chad took special care to say her name with three distinct syllables.

She smiled and half winked one eye. "Chad, you are much too complimentary. I'm merely a file clerk.

They bring me here for display purposes only. What do you do at the embassy, Lieutenant?"

"I'm just a file clerk." Parker didn't have long to wait for a reply.

"And I'm Catherine, the Great."

"All right, I'll confess, I'll confess. The truth is that I help Chad out in the coding room. They put me there once they found out that I couldn't read." There was a pause. Maybe something was lost in the translation so it was time to turn the conversation around. "How do you like London?"

She looked into Chad eyes. "It is too dark and dreary."

"Catherine's from Kiev, it's in the southern part of Russia."

"Thanks, Chad," Parker wanted an excuse to move on. "I'm going to find that waiter with the snails, I'll be right back." He looked for Foxworthy or Evans, but couldn't spot them. He looked back towards Chad. The couple seemed to be talking about something serious. Somehow he felt he didn't fit in tonight. Suddenly, he was looking forward to a quiet evening with Betty.

The procedure was getting to be a routine. Penelope gave him his airline tickets, military transport chits, and a diplomatic passport in his own name. Higgins gave him his gun and added, "Amsterdam…. That ought to be fun." Parker didn't know if that was meant to be a bon voyage message or a warning. He concluded it really didn't matter. The cashier didn't blink an eye as he counted out $2000 in hundreds and twenties.

The bag Smythe handed him was light. Evidently it contained no rotors this time. It was time to travel.

Military transport to Paris was a C-14, which was better known as a DC-3. Parker was the only Navy man on board. There were twelve Army personnel of various ranks. Officers were seated toward the front. Parker's seat became the dividing line between the rankings. The officer going to his seat in front of him was a Second Lieutenant with a very shiny gold bar and no ribbons. He turned around towards Parker.

"What do you have in that bag, swabbie?" he said as he looked down at Parker.

That was enough to irritate Parker. He wasn't about to take any shit from a kid.

"My lunch," Parker snapped. He rotated his gun belt so that the gun was nearly in his lap and looked out the window. He was waiting for a reply so he could stand up, but none came.

The Military Air Transport System (MATS) used the smaller of the two Paris Airports, Le Bourget. Parker got a cab to the Embassy. A staff member recognized him from the last trip. This time he had been assigned a small businessman's hotel just off the Bois de Boulogne and was instructed to retrieve the pouch early the next morning. He made sure he got a written receipt for the pouch. It was a weekday so there was no need for the SOP routine. After checking into the hotel, he took a cab to Montmartre. The Basilica du Sacre Coeur gleamed under the noontime sun.

He stopped in Madame Marie's to see Madeline, but she no longer worked there. Must have found someone with $500 or more, he figured. Or maybe the view of the Sacred Heart Church got to her. Madame Marie offered him the pick of the group, but he thanked her and went back to the hotel. He kept thinking that a quickie, after experiencing Madeline and Penelope, would surely be a let down.

It was time to do some of the souvenir gathering as directed. He stuck to the usual stuff: a metal replica of the Eiffel Tower, a bracelet featuring various landmark charms, and some very racy French Postcards purchased from a street vendor. After a modest outdoor cafe dinner, Parker decided to extend the tourist thing to some nightlife. He found the show at the Follies Bergere had already started and the doors were closed, but there was still a crowd milling around the entrance to the Lido. The doorman was making it clear that he was admitting only people who had reservations. Parker was about to give up, but then reached for his wallet and extracted one of the new $20 bills and cupped it in hand. He waved it shouting in his best French accent, *"Reservation! Reservation!"* The doorman parted the crowd much like Moses did with the Red Sea. The money disappeared in a handshake. He was getting to have more respect for Higgins. Money sure seems to beat guns. At least for now.

After being seated, he was shown the champagne list. He asked for a Heinekens. It would be best to keep a clear head. After all, Smythe emphasized that a lot of people were counting on him.

Rome was spectacular. The military plane touched down at the Leonardo de Vinci Airport in mid morning and it looked like all Italy was bathed in sunshine. The stop at the embassy was routine. He dropped the pouch off at the embassy while he took a short ride to the Vatican for a late lunch at St. Peters Square. He selected a restaurant with outside tables. The size and splendor of the Basilica was breathtaking.

"Number four looks good to me," Parker told the waiter. He had no idea of what was on the menu but he wasn't going to let the waiter know that. The only Italian he could recall was a few swear words accompanied by appropriate hand motions learned at high school.

"Coffee, Signore?"

"Black." The Navy taught him to drink it that way. It was quick, and you didn't have to contend with contaminated sugar or cream. Boiled water would kill everything else.

The waiter turned, but stopped by the next table to take an order from a man seated alone. Couples or foursomes occupied several of the other tables. The singular middle aged man was of dark complexion but did not have the pear shape usually seen in elderly Italian men. His clothes were not well tailored. A Frenchman on holiday, he guessed.

After lunch, Parker visited the street vendor stalls around the square.

"How much is that crucifix?"

"Ten dollars." the vendor replied in nearly perfect English.

"Too much."

"Not for an American Officer. But since you won the war, I can cut the price to eight dollars."

"It's not nice to steal from American liberators."

"It's not nice to try to steal a crucifix from a poor street vendor." He picked up the crucifix and handed it to Parker. "This is the one you want. It was blessed by the Pope."

"How much is it if it is not blessed by the Pope?" Parker quipped still examining the piece.

"Everything here is blessed by the Pope. He blesses everything in the square every Sunday morning."

"Five dollars."

"Seven dollars. That's my best price. Any lower and you would be taking bread out of my children's mouths." He snatched the amulet back.

Parker turned his head for a moment pretending to think. His eye caught the figure of the Frenchman at the next stall. Maybe just a coincidence.

If he was going to spend at least $500 on this trip on souvenirs, he'd better make a deal quickly. He pealed off a $20 that was quickly accepted by the merchant. "I also want these," he said as he picked up a few other trinkets and some post cards.

An audience with the Pope would have been nice, but Parker opted to take the short tour of the Vatican, the Sistine Chapel and the Pieta would have to do.

As Parker exited he was sure he saw the Frenchman reading the newspaper at a seat in a cafe adjacent to the exit door of the Vatican tours. This was no coincidence. About five feet five, dark hair, somewhat curly, small trimmed mustache. fiftyish, sloppy dresser. Something to tell Evans

The Leonardo de Vinci Airport was crowded. It was the height of the tourist season and it seemed everyone wanted to see Rome before they died.

Parker felt reasonably sure that he was not followed, but Antoine was never more than a hundred meters behind him at any time. The Frenchman had been tipped off when Parker entered the Paris Embassy. Trailing Parker around Paris was easy. The taxi trip to the Le Bourget airport, however, told him that Parker's flight would be military and there would be no easy way to track him. A well placed fist full of francs to the tower dispatcher revealed the flight plan to Rome and he was out on the next commercial flight. He picked up the trail outside the American Embassy.

Italian customs waved Parker through. At the military transit desk, the clerk told him there was a change in schedule and directed him towards gate 11. The gate opened right onto the tarmac. Facing Parker was a twin engine Convair painted a camouflage green with its stairs folded out. Parker was sure it was the same plane that he flew from Naples to London, but as he approached he noted it was much older. He climbed the stairs and entered the plane.

"I'm Buzz Adams," the lone occupant said as he extended his hand. "It's about time you got here."

Parker shook his hand. It was callused but not firm. "What's going on?"

"You're Parker, no?"

Parker nodded.

"Well, we've got a lot of ground to cover. I'll fill you in once we're airborne. Why don't you come into the cockpit and keep me company. You're the only passenger."

Adams looked like he had stepped out of a 1930's pulp fiction magazine. He had on nothing close to a uniform and wore a leather helmet with goggles in the up on the forehead position. The airplane looked in terrible condition and the copilot's seat was torn with stuffing extended out at least an inch in several spots.

The engines started with barely a cough and Adams got clearance. He was given the third position for take-off and this gave the engines some time to warm up. Parker tossed his overnight bag and the diplomatic pouch behind the cockpit door and settled into the copilot's seat. He faced a myriad of instruments. His engineering training helped him a bit. RPM, oil pressure, manifold pressure. Parker could clearly see that the manifold pressure on the starboard engine was wiggling around zero while the port engine gage was normal.

"Hey, Buzz. That manifold pressure looks off on the starboard engine. Better check it."

Adams gave it an annoyed look and a look at the engine then back at the gage. He then pushed back enough in his seat to raise his right leg. With an unexpected burst of energy, he slammed his heel directly into the gage. The glass splintered. The gage died.

"What the hell are you doing?" Parker screamed over the noise of the engines. "You crazy or something?"

Buzz got the go ahead from the tower and shoved the throttles full open. The old plane creaked, but the engines roared and the plane jumped forward picking up speed down the runway.

"That fuckin' gage hasn't worked for six months. Now it won't bother you"

Parker gripped the sides of his chair. If he could have figured out how to cut the engines, he would have, but for the moment he just held on.

Every sailor has his own scenario on dying which prepares him for what might happen at sea. The sequence in drowning is quite predictable. You struggle in the water until you are reconciled to your fate. Death comes painlessly. But Parker had no scenario for a painful ending in an airplane. He was temporality frozen stiff with unexpected fear as the plane accelerated.

The plane trundled ahead, bounced a few times, then lifted skyward. Buzz banked the plane steeply to the left and headed North.

At about 6000 feet Buzz backed off on the throttles and Parker relaxed a bit as the noise of the engines lessened.

"About that crazy part," Buzz said, "you're right. I'm the only one crazy enough to do things like this."

"Like what?"

"We're going up the west coast of Italy for awhile. Then we sink to about 500 feet to stay below the Trieste radar and drop into a small patch of green just outside of Udine. They want you to meet someone there. Only a crazy man would do this."

"Where are the parachutes?"

"They wouldn't do you any good from 500 feet."

"Where's your uniform? Are you Army or CIA?"

"Just Army. Major Adams. And I do just about anything I want as long as I do everything they want."

Parker just took another deep breath, held it, then let it out slowly.

"Yeah, I've got only a year left before retirement. I flew A20A's during the war. You know, those fast, low-level attack bombers. You learned more how to fly by watching the terrain than by instruments. I'm their perfect hero for getting into small, obscure places."

"Well, I feel a lot better now that I know that you have some flying experience," Parker responded trying to lighten up a little. "But what's with the helmet?"

"Once one of these Convairs I was flying blew a window out. I nearly froze and went blind before I got control of the plane. This way I just flip the goggles down in case it happens. It adds a little character around the airports and the women just love it. I have a thermos in the back if you want some coffee. I'd recommend you pass since we don't have a First Class section lavatory in this craft."

As Parker relaxed a little, the drone of the plane's engines became hypnotic. In a clouded image he saw the back of a woman disrobing. It couldn't be Madeline. She had already left him. It must be Penelope. The dream was interrupted by turbulence.

They were passing through the clouds on their decent to 500 feet. They were over water, but there were few ships. The Adriatic was the most dangerous waterway in the world. Mines from WWII were not yet removed completely so ships moved slowly and on a precision course. Their flight path was North passing about half way between Venice and Trieste. Adams cut the speed back slightly below cruising level taking the aircraft even lower. The coastline was ahead, but neither of the cities was visible. Over land the landscape became a blur to Parker. Adams seemed to be tense, but in control.

"We're looking for the church steeple at Udine," Adams informed Parker.

Parker looked ahead, then left, right. "There's something white out to the right."

Adams banked sharply. He caught sight of the spire. "That's it. You make a good navigator, Parker."

Adams banked sharply left and a small strip of grass appeared. He steered directly for the target. It had a half dozen cows grazing in the field. He appeared to be settling in over the field when he reached over and shoved the throttles wide open. The engines roared and the cattle scattered out of the way. A man ran out shaking his fist as they banked for another run.

"It's all part of an act. If he doesn't run out and make a scene, we don't land. Hang on. We're going in on a grass runway full of cow shit."

Adams brought the craft in with all the grace of an air circus pilot from the depression era. He was right about the landing being rough. Parker thought sure the landing gear would come off, but it didn't. The plane ran to the end of the strip and turned around. Adams turned the port engine off, but left the starboard engine running. The man who was shaking his fist was now driving a tractor hauling a tank on a wagon towards the plane. There was another man riding on the rear of the wagon.

"We have to refuel to make it to Munich. Be quick about what you have to do. We need to get through the mountains before we lose the light."

Parker didn't know what he had to do. He did know enough to flick the safety off on his pistol.

Adams opened the door and let the stairs down. Buzz jumped on the wing and the man handed the nozzle to him. He returned to the wagon and started up a small gasoline motor working a pump. The man on the back of the wagon jumped off and came towards the plane. Parker came down the stairs. He felt he was safer outside the plane while it was being fueled in case there was any gunfire. Not taking any chances Parker unclipped his holster top and put his hand firmly on the gun. He still had the key to the NATO plans and wasn't about to lose them on some cow pasture in Italy if he could help it.

There was still plenty of light. The man approaching the plane was small and very dark complexioned. Parker could now see his features. He was Serbian. Some of Parker's schoolmates in Ohio were Serbian. He was sure of it.

His clothes were clean but worn. He slowed as he approached Parker. He showed one hand empty, but held a small box in the other.

"Parker," he spoke in a deep accent. "I have this for you."

"Hand it over very slowly." Parker gripped the pistol handle tighter with his right hand as he reached for the box with his left. It was not heavy. He kept his eye on the man's eyes, looking for a clue as to what he might do.

"Do you have anything for me?" he asked not changing his body position.

Parker quickly searched his brain for a clue. Smythe didn't tell him a thing about this.

"No, not this time," Parker answered as if he had been instructed.

"We're all set, Parker," yelled Adams. Finish your business and let's get out of here."

The man facing Parker turned slowly and started to walk away. Parker wanted to call him back and give him some money or something, but knew he couldn't.

The takeoff was no less bumpy than the landing. They seemed to brush the top of the trees, but Adams didn't appear concerned at all. Parker still held the box in his hand. It wasn't sealed so he opened it. It was a small, inexpensive music box, the kind you could find in most any souvenir shop. He lifted the lid and it played a tune he could not recognize. He wound it up and played it again.

"Aida," Buzz stated as he threaded the plane through the Alps towards Munich.

* * *

The private telephone line in Boris Chernoff's office rang. Only the most urgent calls came over this line. From the East it would be scrambled and most certainly be from Moscow. Calls from the West would be clear language but contain codes. He turned rapidly and snatched the phone.

"Section 65 Chief Chernoff," he barked the identification code for the day.

"Boris, I saw your new friend Thursday," the voice on the phone stated.

The words were in French in a measured cadence. Boris immediately recognized Antoine's voice. The slowness was calculated to let Boris take in everything so nothing would have to be repeated, but Antoine did not comprehend Chernoff's mastery of the language. *He had spotted Parker.*

"Did he have anything to say?"

"He's on holiday. He's visiting Brussels, Paris, and Rome. Other than that his plans are indefinite."

The first mention of a sequence is ignored. *He was spotted in Paris, but lost him in Rome somewhere. Nothing unusual in his routine so far.*

"Good, you probably will see him again. If you do, let him know I'm going on holiday myself, maybe we can get together somewhere for a drink."

Antoine read that quickly. *Pick up his trail and follow him. Let him know that you are around. Chernoff may want to get involved.*

"All right. How's the weather in Berlin?"

It was time to cut the conversation. Antoine had his orders.

"Fine, just fine."

Boris placed the phone in its cradle. It was time to put some pressure on that son of a bitch Evans. If Parker was indeed their only courier now, he was the weak link in the CIA information chain. Things had been too peaceful for those bastards. Once Parker was found, he'd have some fun with him.

CHAPTER EIGHT

The stopover in Munich was just long enough to visit the men's room. Parker was slated to take the next military transport to Bonn. The delivery to the American Embassy in West Germany's capital city went without incident. Parker squeezed in enough time to pick up a beer stein and a small music box to add to his souvenir collection. Brussels was boring, but Amsterdam was a totally different situation as Higgins had subtlety inferred.

"Technically you are the only military officer on duty in the city," a low-level attaché at the American Embassy in Amsterdam informed Parker. "We have no military presence here, but Amsterdam has become a favorite R and R spot for American military personnel from all over Europe. The Dutch take a rather casual attitude towards drugs and prostitution is legalized. As Senior Officer Present, you will be expected to answer all police calls for assistance that involve the military. The local police will be very cooperative."

"Thanks a bunch," Parker replied. He was not looking forward to this.

Paris was a cakewalk compared to Amsterdam. No sooner than he had checked into his room at the Grand Karapinski Hotel, the telephone rang.

"Lieutenant, this is Chief of Police of the fourteenth district. We have a problem with a Marine in the Windmill Cafe. I'm sending a Jeep with two of our men around in five minutes. You will be in charge."

The Windmill was in a relatively quiet section of Amsterdam and definitely not a tourist trap bar. Parker entered with the two burly policemen behind him. Eight Dutchmen had surrounded an American soldier who had his back to the Jukebox. He had a drink in one hand and a beer bottle held by its neck with the other. It looked like an unfair fight to Parker.

The bartender slid from behind the bar and went directly to Parker.

"Do something! They are going to kill him."

"What's going on here?" Parker shouted trying to get everyone's attention.

The policemen shouted something in Dutch and the crowd seemed to ease a little.

The bartender spoke up, "The Marine keeps playing the same song. The customers are sick of it. If he doesn't stop, they threatened to kill him!"

Parker parted the crowd and got closer to the corporal. It was obvious that the soldier had been drinking, but did not appear drunk.

"I think it's time to move on, soldier. This situation is starting to turn ugly."

"I'm not budging. I'm in Europe to protect liberty, and I will play the 'The Yellow Rose of Texas' as long as I want. Free speech is guaranteed by the constitution. All these foreigners can go to hell." He moved to the side putting his glass down and dropped another coin in the Jukebox, not taking his gaze off Parker.

All the eyes in the bar were on Parker. The two policemen had their clubs in their hands. Parker was seething. It's not nice to lecture and screw around with the Ultimate Supreme Commander of the United States Armed forces in the area.

Parker took another step closer to the soldier and said softly, "You might just be right, soldier."

The corporal relaxed a moment. That was his mistake.

Without changing his expression, Parker swiftly grabbed the soldier by both lapels as tightly as he could and drove him hard back into the juke box at the same time raising his knee into the soldier's crotch. The bottle dropped. The soldier tried to bend over from the blow, but Parker wouldn't let him go.

"But not this time." He turned the corporal around and pushed him toward the policemen. He then went to the Jukebox and yanked the cord out of the wall with such force that it snapped the cord.

"Did they teach you at move in da Navy?" asked one of the policemen as they helped the soldier into the rear seat of the Jeep.

"Nope. I learned it in high school." Parker wasn't sure they understood. "If this guy's leave papers are in order, we'll take him a couple of blocks and drop him off. After that, we'll head back to the hotel."

"We already have a trouble call from Warmoesstraat. You may not get back to the hotel for quite some time."

"We'll see about that," Parker countered. He'd taken care of the first call in a few minutes; he could settle the next just as quickly. He couldn't have been more wrong.

Warmoesstraat Street is the heart of the legalized prostitution business. It's different from Paris. The French do things in a more subtle fashion but with an understanding of some protocol. The Dutch prostitution process is more like a supermarket. The houses have large windows where the ladies display their fancy parts and go through gyrations to attract customers. It's competition in close proximity. It seems the expectations are brought to a much higher level than the verbal solicitation used by the French.

The first call in the district was about a non-payment for services. The soldier had a difference of opinion as to what services he was to receive. The vendor claimed the requested services were rendered. The pimp was detaining the soldier but was physically no match to force the payment.

Parker was getting tired. Prostitution was legal. Not paying was illegal. It was simple.

Parker made a command decision. "Arrest the son-of-a-bitch."

No one argued. After all they already had another call. A "Marine" was pissing on the front steps of one of the whorehouses. It was going to be a long night.

At 0900 the magistrate came into chambers. Everyone stood. Eleven hung over enlisted men from various branches of the United States of America Armed Forces struggled to get to their feet. They were a rag-tag bunch with most of their uniforms stained with vomit or other bodily fluids

Parker stepped forward. "All the men have agreed to plead guilty. The prosecutor and I have agreed to suggest a twenty-dollar fine in US currency plus any specific damages to property. As Senior Officer Present I am representing them, I enter an apology for each of the men."

The magistrate looked slowly with disgust over the motley bunch then slammed his gavel. It was over.

Copenhagen was on Parker's schedule for three nights and four days. He remembered his instructions well "Get familiar with the town; buy souvenirs." Penelope scheduled Parker into one of the best hotels near the center of town. The choice of the Neptune was her idea of humor. It turned out to be a fine choice.

Parker shifted to civilian clothes and arranged for a quick tour of the city at the concierge desk to get his bearings. The city seemed to be largely spared by the war. He particularly liked the parks and had no trouble engaging people in conversation since almost everyone spoke English.

With the pouch secure at the Embassy, Parker started to relax. In the evening, he explored the Tivoli Gardens and took his evening meals there. During the day, he carefully noted the street names and landmarks that may be useful in the future and established his favorite bars and cafes. He made conversation with the room maids and bellboys. Where are the best bars and cafes? Where are the best nightclubs? He took a cab.

"Just drive around the city and show me the sights," Parker instructed.

"Your first trip to Copenhagen?"

"Yes, I may be doing some business here soon. What's your name?"

"Eric."

"Is Copenhagen your home town?"

"Yes. Do you expect to do a lot of entertaining."

"Probably not, but I want to know my way around."

"You have the right cabby."

They spent an hour driving, stopping, looking and chatting. Parker asked Eric about the major buildings and shops.

"That's enough for today, Eric. Back to the Neptune. Pick me up tomorrow at the same time. I'll buy lunch."

Parker spent the next hour in the Neptune cocktail lounge making notes. He made a special note of Eric's telephone number. He could use him if he was going to make Copenhagen a regular stop.

* * *

"Coffee or tea, sir?"

Boris Chernoff looked up from the dossier. "Coffee."

The propeller driven aircraft was noisy and uncomfortable, but it was the only available transportation from Berlin to Copenhagen on such short notice.

The folder on Parker was thin. No photograph was available. The physical description was commonplace and could have fit a million Americans. From a town in Ohio called Cleveland. Must have been named after a President, Chernoff vaguely recalled. No record of his father. Mother remarried and is employed in the postal service. No other family members identified. Graduated from a college in Ohio. Service record in the Navy was clean and unspectacular. No indication of any special training. The lack of detailed information made Chernoff doubly suspicious that he might be dealing with a highly trained agent.

Agent Antoine Dione had contacted Chernoff shortly after he was informed that Parker had made contact with the American Embassy in Copenhagen. He had tailed him for a day. Chernoff wanted to take a closer look.

Chernoff considered the Frenchman one of his top agents. Dione had been a minor official in the French Communist Party before the war, but considered himself a loyal Frenchman above all else. He joined the French Resistance movement almost immediately after Hitler established the Vichy regime. When it came to blowing up train tracks the Germans were using for transportation, he became an expert in the cloak and dagger end of the operation. When the war ended, de Gaulle stepped in so quickly that there was little hope of establishing a viable communist faction in the government. Robbed of learning a productive trade, he took menial jobs to earn a living. A contact at the Russian Embassy in Paris gave him an offer he couldn't resist. For a monthly package of Francs, he was to be an operative, taking instructions from the Russian KGB section in East Berlin.

Antoine met Boris as he disembarked from the morning flight from Berlin. He firmly shook the hand of his friend and superior in the party. Chernoff responded with a Russian hug as they started to talk about Parker.

"He seems to be just doing the tourist things. No particular pattern to his path. He has made no contacts with known or suspected agents. No obvious drops were made. We searched his hotel room and found nothing. His pouch and gun must be at the Embassy. He seems to have picked out the Cafeen Nikolaj for his late lunches. If he is true to form, you can get a look at him there."

It was nearly 1 p.m. when they left by taxi.

Antoine signaled the taxi driver to stop. "We must walk the rest of the way," Antoine said as he paid the fare.

Boris nodded. It was bright and clear and he was enjoying his day in the sun. There is never enough sun in Berlin and it's even worse in mother Russia, Chernoff reflected.

The tables were only half occupied as they approached. Antoine grabbed Chernoff's arm and jerked his head towards a table where a single man in a light gray suit was seated. The man was talking to the waiter. Antoine steered Chernoff to a table at Parker's back.

Dashal Koenig made a decision to be a waiter while looking upward from a canvas floor. He was large for a Dane and made a brief attempt to be a boxer, but his opponent in his first professional bout outmatched his strength with pugilistic skills. Waiting tables was a lot more fun and the money was good. He stood at Parker's table ready to take an order.

"The steak sandwich is very good today, Mr. Parker," the waiter said. "Our chef says it is very special."

"Well, if he recommends it, Dashal, I'll have to try it. Make that medium and bring me some coffee, black." Parker was glad to try beef whenever he could. The English couldn't stand importing beef from the continental Europeans so they settled for mutton as their staple. It was usually tough and had the taste of grass.

Dashal and Parker struck it off from their first meeting. Parker came in after the noon rush and he tipped well above the service already added to the check. Dashal was free with information on where to go and what to do. Today, when Parker arrived, Dashal took him to a table he seemed to favor and had it set up for him.

Boris took a good look at Parker who seemed very relaxed. "He looks very young. You say he just sits here and has lunch, no contacts of any sort. Very strange."

Antoine nodded his head.

"What about the waiter?"

"My guess is that he is clean. He's Danish and has worked here for several years. Makes good tips. I've never seen anything pass between them."

"I think it's time to put some pressure on him."

"You should find this to your liking, sir," Dashal said as he placed the steak sandwich in front of Parker. He laid the steak knife across the back of the plate. "Any special plans for today?"

"No, I have a late afternoon flight to London. All I need to do is finish a little shopping. Any suggestions?"

"Stay on the Stroget. All the best shops are there. If you are looking for something expensive, I'd suggest some Royal Copenhagen porcelain figurines. If you're just looking for less expensive, small statues of *The Little Mermaid* are always a good choice."

97

"Thanks."

"Bon appetite."

Chernoff rose from his chair and strode nonchalantly towards Parker's table. He timed his approach so as Parker was taking his first bite of the steak, he pulled the chair out and said, "Do you mind if I join you?"

Before Parker could swallow and speak, Boris had taken his seat directly opposite him.

"Well, I wasn't exactly expecting anyone," Parker said trying to remain friendly. He looked over his intruder. Stout, dressed in a poor quality suit, spoke clearly with just a touch of an English accent.

"We know who you are."

"Well, that's nice," Parker quipped now thinking this was some kind of joke.

"We know what you are doing," the man said with a steely-eyed look that sent the message that this was no laughing matter.

Parker's body kicked into the fight or flight mode quickly. He didn't know what was going on here, but a quick exit looked like the most discreet thing to do. He slowly put down his knife and fork, then brought the napkin up with his right hand while pushing away from the table with his left.

Chernoff's right hand darted across the table grabbing Parker's left wrist. Years of hard farm labor on the steppes had not been lost in the months behind a desk in Berlin. Parker winced. It was like his hand was in a vice bolted to the table. The pain was so great it took his breath away. He slowly sank back into his chair. It was done so smoothly no one seemed to notice. Chernoff slowly released his grip.

"This won't take long, Parker. We are not really interested in what you are doing now."

Parker was seething from within. He didn't like being bullied. His left wrist felt like it was broken, but probably just sprained. His pulse was beating a tattoo in his brain. He tried to give some semblance of calmness by breathing slowly, but was doing a bad job of it. He sat up straight in his seat so that he was taller than Chernoff who was now leaning in towards him and speaking more softly.

"We have searched your room. You are nothing but a delivery boy. But somewhere along the line, you will be handling very sensitive material that we may be interested in. Now we could take that from you at any time, but this would cut off our options in the future. We would rather have a more on-going relationship. We would like a little cooperation. You would do your job; we would do ours. Nothing would be taken or altered. We will make copies or take your word for any information you might tell us. You could be a rich man."

Parker continued to look directly at Chernoff who now took on a more relaxed attitude as he leaned on the table.

"I know they pay poorly in the Navy."

That pushed Parker's button. *You son-of-a-bitch.* With a single motion he grabbed the steak knife which was lying on his plate and drove it downward right towards Chernoff's left wrist. Surprised, Chernoff backed off quickly but the knife drove into the table catching Chernoff's suit coat sleeve, ripping it as he drew back.

"Kiss my ass!" were the only words Parker could think of.

The few patrons at the cafe turned, and Dashal rushed over to the table as Parker and Chernoff faced off against each other across the table.

The Dane was the imposing figure in this standoff towering above both of them. "Any problem, Mr. Parker?"

"No," Parker slowly answered as Chernoff rose, backed away, turned, and vanished down the street. A figure darted past Parker and headed in the same direction. It looked like the Frenchman, but Parker could only see his back so he couldn't be sure.

"Nice move with that knife, Mr. Parker. Where did you learn that?"

"In high school," Parker responded as if by rote. It was a lie. He learned to trust a knife to protect his bowling alley earnings as a pinsetter when he was 15. "Bring me some ice in a towel. That son-of-a-bitch ruined my lunch."

"I'll bring another steak sandwich right away," Dashal said in consolation as he struggled to loosen the knife from the table.

At precisely 0900, Parker entered Penelope's office carrying a gym bag.

"Have a good trip, James?"

"Just fine. Brought you something from Copenhagen," Parker teased gesturing towards the bag. Then he sat on her desk and leaned across to give her a kiss, but she dodged the move successfully.

"Behave yourself, James. We're just friends, you know."

That was something he didn't want to be reminded of. Evidently, she had not changed her mind. "Just something for setting me up at the Neptune. Great hotel." He partially opened the bag giving her a glimpse of porcelain Royal Copenhagen Ballerina figurine.

"Pleased to be able to help, but you shouldn't have."

"It's not yours yet. I have to clear it through naval customs first," Parker said as he motioned towards Foxworthy's office.

"The captain is at a meeting, but Commander Smythe is waiting for you in his office. Go right away."

Parker emptied the contents of his bag slowly one at a time onto Smythe's desk. The items added to the already cluttered desk. He left the two music boxes for last. The German box came out first, then he paused for a reaction. Smythe sat there without changing an iota of his expression. Timing a two-second delay to add some suspense, Parker then took the music box from Udine and extended it towards Smythe.

"Lieutenant Parker," Smythe started sarcastically. "You may think you are funny, but you are not. We don't have time to fuck around here." He examined the music box quickly. "Get up to see Evans right now. They're planning to keep you so busy you won't have time to wipe your own ass."

Parker expected a little more relaxed atmosphere since Foxworthy wasn't there, but obviously there must be more pressure on the Embassy than he had thought.

Pointing toward the porcelain ballerina, Parker asked, "Commander, I wonder if I could have......."

Smythe cut him off, "You're excused, Lieutenant."

Parker snapped to attention, saluted, and spun around. Penelope would be pissed.

CHAPTER NINE

Normally, the back wall of Evans' office was draped with an opening just wide enough to accommodate a photograph of the current president. Now, it was fully opened revealing cork boards on either side. Foxworthy had just finished pinning a large, detailed map of Norway to the left-hand board.

"Even though the bulk of the fleet is over in the Pacific dealing with that Korean mess, the Sixth Fleet in the Med should be able to bottle up any Russian ships by sealing off the Bosporous. NATO's order of battle is to have the Army plan fall back and hold Italy at the Alps while the main force performs a delaying action in France."

"Sounds like a re-run of 1914 and 1940," Evans commented.

"Yes, but this time the good guys have virtually no naval presence in the North Sea. The US has only a single destroyer in the North Sea making a goodwill tour, but we do have a reasonable number of submarines still stationed in the North Atlantic. I have the OK for two more destroyers, which have recently been re-commissioned and refitted with the most sophisticated jet plane defense systems."

"How do we fit in?"

"The destroyers' mission will be to provide some air cover where needed, but primarily they would transport critical materials or personnel while we are in the fall back mode. Our subs should be able to discourage any large Russian ships from leaving

Leningrad so we don't expect any surface engagements. Air attacks are another thing. If things get hot, we need places for the destroyers to duck into and hide. The fjords of Norway are ideal but we lack crucial details. Parker has destroyer experience and we want to send him in to look around. What we need is photography equipment, a cover story, and a plan to get Parker in to obtain the information we need without getting the Norwegians antsy."

"I think we can whip that up in a hurry. What's your time schedule?"

The conversation was interrupted by the intercom. "Lieutenant Parker is coming in as requested, Mr. Evans."

As Parker entered, he saw the two men standing near the map. Neither man smiled.

"I assume you retrieved the music box without incident," Evans stated.

"The flight was a little bumpy, but I got the box back OK. It would have been nice to know that I had a pickup to make. Something happened in Copenhagen that you both should know about."

"Later," Foxworthy snapped cutting Parker off. "We have a priority emergency assignment for you. Listen up." Foxworthy motioned Parker to the map.

"We're increasing our destroyer count here to three next week. We're worried about protecting them in case the Russians get frisky. The fjords of Norway are excellent places for the tin cans to duck into for protection. We have maps in great detail as you can see, but we lack information on topography. We need to know how steep the sides rise in fjords where the destroyers could hide. If the slopes are steep enough, they will limit detection and provide some cover from air attack. Your experience should come into play here."

Parker moved in closer to the map.

"We are looking at about a dozen places from Bremen to Alesund where there might be protection from air attacks." Foxworthy drew his finger over the coastline. "We need you to go in there undercover and pick out the best fjords. Ones with steep sides but not so long that the cans couldn't get out quickly if necessary. The destroyers are the same class as the Perry, so we expect you to use some judgment.

"Sir, maybe I'm missing something. Why the undercover part? The Norwegians are members of NATO, why don't we just ask them to get the information and save me the trip?"

"If we did, the Norwegians would ask to see the whole plan and right now we don't think they would be happy with what they would see."

"You mean we would offer them little or no aid during the initial move of the Russians."

"I'd prefer you stay out of strategic planning and stick to your assignments," Evans broke in. "We don't feel Norwegian security is tight enough to handle extremely sensitive information." He had already conjured up a plan for the assignment. "We have a camera that should do the trick, but you'll need some instruction. Documents identifying you as a National Geographic photographer will be an excellent cover. Language should be no problem since almost everyone speaks some English. We can have you ready to leave the day after tomorrow. Get some civilian clothes that will match the assignment and bill them to us. You won't have much time. Now, tell us what happened in Copenhagen."

When Parker finished reporting on the incident at the Copenhagen cafe, there was silence. He had left out the part about the knife, but included some extra emphasis on the "Kiss my ass" part.

Evans finally spoke, "Obviously they are watching the Embassies. You say they told you they searched your hotel room?"

"At first I didn't believe them. None of the souvenirs were missing, but my shaving kit was the giveaway. It was exactly in the same place I left it, but the deodorant stick was on its edge. I always lay it flat on the bottom. Just an engineering idiosyncrasy."

"Well, we've got to change a few things. Don't change your routines when coming in or out of the Embassy in uniform. Take most of your civilian clothes over to Conrad's place. You two are buddies, no?"

Parker nodded yes knowing full well that they were monitoring their escapades.

"We'll have to give you some tips on evasive action to lose any tails, but all assignments in civilian clothes will be out of his flat from now on. At this time they are probably just watching the Embassy. The assumption about your not knowing much was logical. We'll try to keep it that way."

Foxworthy took over. With his finger, he traced a circle around the southern third of Norway. "We'll have this section of the map enlarged for you. Higgins will take care of the technical details. Work with Penelope on travel arrangements. Use some imagination. We need good data and we need it in a hurry. Two weeks, Parker, is all you have. Any questions?"

"It sounds simple enough, sir."

It was late morning when Parker entered Selfridges first floor. The store was not crowded. He looked around for an information board, but couldn't spot one so he turned toward the elevator figuring that there may be one nearby. Walking through the Women's Wear Department, he came full faced toward a pair of shapely legs at eye level. They belonged to a young woman standing on a step stool adjusting clothing on a mannequin placed on an elevated display.

Parker came to a stop as the young woman started to descend from the wobbling step stool. He extended his hand. "Can I steady you?" he asked.

"Thanks for the help," she replied as she turned around and used his hand to keep her balance.

Parker made a quick study. Her stocking seams were straight. Dress was a simple black design. She had about the fairest skin he had ever seen. Her hair was almost pitch black, short, and neatly arranged. No rings. Strikingly beautiful.

"Well, maybe you can help me," Parker said quickly while still holding her hand. "I'm looking for the Men's Department. I need some casual clothes and maybe some hiking gear in a hurry. Can you give me some direction?" He added a smile.

"Third floor, take the lift." She slowly withdrew her hand. Parker's hand felt good to her. It was warm and firm, but not callused. He looked like an officer and, more importantly to her, a gentleman. "I'm headed that way. Let me show you."

The young woman walked slightly ahead of Parker.

"What's all that gold braid for?"

"That means that I'm very important. My name's James Parker." He looked down at her nametag. "Miss Reynolds. You must have a first name."

"It's Airy."

"Airy? What kind of name is that?"

"It means I'm a very important person," she replied with a smile. She paused to be sure that Parker got the humor.

"There's got to be more to it than that." They had reached the elevator, but Parker blocked her way. She didn't seem to mind.

"It's short for Harriet"

"What do you do here?"

"I'm a buyer for women's clothing. I help out dressing up displays as you saw. I occasionally model women's wear when they get desperate."

The elevator door opened; the light indicated it was headed down to the basement level. She gracefully sidestepped Parker and entered.

"Third floor?" he asked.

"Third floor."

"Maybe I'll see you again," Parker said. "Selfridges is my favorite store." The door began to close.

"Administration."

It was a message he wouldn't forget.

The camera was large and had a long lens protruding from the body. Parker and CIA Specialist Albert Whitehall bent over the instrument.

"This looks like a standard camera that a naturalist would be using," Whitehall explained. "The long lens is telescopic so you can take photos from considerable distances. What makes this camera different is that it has a grid overlaid which ties into the focus so we can calculate the slope and height of the sides of the fjords from the photographs. Be sure you take at least two photos at each location at as close to 90 degrees as you can so we can do some triangulation. You will be using a high-speed black and white 35-mm film. The f-stop openings will be adjusted manually in accordance to the chart that is pasted on the camera. I want you to take a half dozen or so shots here so we are sure you have the hang of it. Try some shots of the next building, then some of the park. Do you have a camera yourself?"

"I've got an Argus C3 that takes some great slides."

"Good. Then you know how important the f stop settings are. In one sense this camera is easier to use than your C3. It's a reflex camera which simply means what you see is exactly what you get."

"No parallax."

Whitehall nodded. He began to feel more at ease knowing that Parker had some camera experience.

Whitehall's work was mainly inside the Embassy where photographic methods of handling data were involved. Miniature cameras for copying documents were currently the big item. Most of his work involved teaching camera techniques to obtain the sharpest image. The success of a mission often hinged upon photographs. If the photos from this assignment were useless, it would be both their asses.

Parker took the camera to the window. He focused the camera onto a building about a half-mile away. The image was remarkably clear and the grid overlaid the entire side of the structure.

"You should adjust the f stop first. It's an overcast day, so make the stop at 5.6. A shutter speed of at least 1/250 is necessary since you are at long distance hand held. With a tripod you can use 1/125 to increase the depth of field. Do you see where to make those adjustments?"

He consulted the table on the camera. The setting of 5.6 matched *overcast*. All the days were overcast in England. He adjusted the shutter speed as suggested, showed it to Whitehall, who approved and then snapped the shot. He tried several others focusing mainly on buildings then lastly on landscapes.

"That's enough. You seem to have the hang of it. One tip. Use a tripod whenever possible. It gets the sharpest pictures and also makes you look professional. Where you can't use one, bring your left elbow into your chest as you hold the camera." Whitehall demonstrated. "This will steady it. I'll show you how to rewind and unload the film. We'll have this film developed in the lab in the next hour just to be sure you did it right. Here's a photographer's bag to make you look authentic. Twenty rolls of 36-exposure film should be plenty. As a rule of thumb, I want you to shoot twice as many shots as you think necessary. There's a small lead-lined bag inside for protecting the exposed film. Once you've shot a roll don't let it out of your sight."

Parker rummaged through the bag.

"All the rolls are numbered," Whitehall continued. "Use them in numerical order and keep good notes on what you shot. You can have 720 good shots, but if you can't relate them to a particular spot or topic, they're useless. We need shots in focus, properly exposed, and identified. OK?"

"Piece of cake."

"Good luck. Higgins is waiting for you."

"Whitehall's a pain in the ass," Higgins related. "He's a TS, you know."

"I assume that means tough shit," Parker said.

"It stands for Technical Specialist. He means well. Comes from a rich family. Yale grad, I think. As an agent, he folded under pressure on his first assignment so they pigeon holed him inside the compound. He takes this photography thing very seriously."

"Maybe that comes from inhaling developing fluid fumes," Parker responded.

"The boss says you will be traveling in casual clothes, so the shoulder holster won't do," Higgins continued. He picked up a small revolver from the table and held it out. "This is the one we normally issue for work of this sort."

Parker studied the revolver. "I'm just getting used to the .45. Where's the holster."

"This is a .22 caliber. The good news is that I've never known this particular model to jam. The bad news is that the small caliber means you'll probably need to hit your target at least twice to stop him. As for the holster, this is it." Higgins handed Parker a piece of twine about 8 inches long. The ends were waxed to keep them from unraveling.

"You've got to be kidding."

"Definitely not. Here, let me show you how to do this." Higgins quickly made a bight in the string. He grabbed a belt loop on Parker's right side pulling the string around it and pulling the free end through the bight then pulled it taut. "Now I'll take it around the belt loop in front and tie a slip knot." He flipped the string inside his pants. "Put the revolver in."

The gun felt cold as Parker carefully placed it in the string holster. "Sort of like an inside joke on John Wayne. It feels like it's aimed at my balls."

"Not to worry. Although there's no safety on this gun, it takes more pressure than you would think to fire the gun. The trigger action will rotate the cylinder one position just before the firing pin comes down. You can cock the gun, but I'd definitely recommend that you not do that. We'll take a few shots down in the range just to be sure you have the feel of it. Also, most of the agents carry this gun in the small of their back. Less of a bulge. Try a couple of positions until you feel comfortable."

Parker felt complimented. Higgins never made a reference to him as an agent before. Maybe he had graduated.

"One more thing, The slip knot is so you can get rid of the "holster" and the gun quickly if you need to dump it somewhere. Some of these European countries are prickly about a foreigner carrying a gun."

Parker looked at the gun. "Neat. Let's see if I can hit the target with this one."

Higgins smiled. He was getting to like this kid.

CHAPTER TEN

The flight to Bergen was short, barely enough time for Parker to look over his documents. The U.S. passport was under the name of Josh Parkinson. Smythe had told him that most of his aliases would have similar sounding names to his own so he could easily respond when spoken to. Parkinson was some kind of disease; Parker mused hoping it wasn't an omen. The National Geographic identification card with his photo looked authentic enough. He had plenty of money, a camera, a gun, and an open air line ticket from Trondheim to Bergen and back to London. The London-Bergen flight was scheduled only twice a week. He would have to keep that in mind to stay within his two-week time allotment.

The day before the trip, Parker moved most of his civilian clothes into Conrad's flat. Chad made another double date with two of the female clerks at the Embassy for that evening. It was Parker's second date with Betty. Dinner at a local pub got enough beer into the girls to make them friendly, then the pairs split to their respective apartments. Betty was fun and laughed a lot but there was no chemistry so there was no likelihood of a third date.

Parker wasn't sure that Conrad was in the loop so he was particularly careful not to mention anything about the upcoming assignment but did tell him that he would be gone for a couple of weeks. The next morning after Chad left for work, he changed into his civilian clothes in Chad's flat and left for the airport three hours ahead of departure time. Traveling light with only the photography bag and a medium sized backpack, he took the Metro, rapidly switching trains before hailing a cab to Heathrow. He wanted no part of being tailed this time if he could help it.

The plane made a rough landing at Bergen. Passing through customs and immigration was without incident. Parker grabbed a cab from the airport and told the driver to head toward the waterfront. Smythe was right. It seemed that everyone spoke English so he had no trouble in locating a ferry that headed North. He bought a ticket on Hurtigruten Line to Alesund, casually mentioning to the clerk that he was a photographer and interested in fjords.

"The ferry leaves tomorrow morning at 7:00 sharp," the clerk said. "It makes a lot of stops along the way. You can get off and on anywhere along the route and get back on later at no extra charge. Just keep your ticket. We run north on Monday, Wednesday, and Friday."

"Can you recommend a hotel for tonight that's not too expensive?"

"Yes. The Rosenkrantz. You can walk there if you want. I'll write out the directions."

It was a perfect day. The mountains in the background made a spectacular scene. The air was crisp and clear. Parker walked leisurely taking in the sights of the town. It also gave him time to see if anyone was following him. He spotted no one.

The Rosenkrantz Hotel was just what he was looking for, convenient and not too flashy. Trying to blend in, he easily struck up a conversation with the concierge who was free with advice on what to do around town. "The best way to get a view of the city is to take the funicular to Floien. You can take wonderful pictures there for your magazine," he said.

Parker spent the rest of the day testing out his camera. He had $3000 worth of US and Norwegian currency plus a day of bright sunshine. Everything seemed to be right. Even the pistol seemed to mold into the small of his back. He started to relax.

* * *

June 17, 1953 was not a good day for Boris Chernoff. Operations in Berlin were chaotic. After days of heated negotiations between German construction labor leaders and their Russian overseers on issues of increasing daily work quotas, the new levels were unilaterally imposed. The union workers promptly walked off the job. Several other unions supported them by also going on strike. The Russians, whose policy was to maintain strict control of occupied East Germany, underestimated German resolve and were totally caught off guard.

Chernoff was not directly involved. His responsibility was intelligence gathering through agents outside of Berlin. Most of the Russian Embassies in Europe routinely sent information from field agents to his office to be evaluated before passing them on to Moscow. Currently the priority assignments involved collecting information on US armed forces concentrations, but they also were on the alert for any information pertaining to East Germany.

"The situation at Karlshorst is getting out of control. Crowds gathered at six this morning chanting for abolishing work quotas, free elections, and a united Berlin." Colonel Fadeikin's face was ashen as he addressed the meeting of the division heads. He had been up all night monitoring the demonstrations and had ordered Russian tanks to quietly move into key areas of East Berlin. "Moscow considers the incidents of the last two days extremely serious. The situation is tense, but not unmanageable. We have been instructed to take quick, punitive measures to identify and arrest the instigators of these demonstrations." He paused for effect. "They are sending Comrade Beria here directly to oversee these operations."

The mere mention of Beria, the dreaded NKVD chief, put chills in everyone. His reputation for ruthlessness was legend. There was absolute silence in the room.

"Comrade Chernoff, we feel that these uprisings are being fueled by American CIA or British MI6. Are there reports from Paris and London to confirm any of this?"

Chernoff had to choose his words well. The Berlin resident chief would like to blame the uprising on the Americans, but Chernoff felt strongly that this was strictly a German ground swell. They had had enough crap from the Russians, and the imposition of increased quotas was the last straw. How dare the Russians, who had demonstrated complete incompetence in running anything, tell the Germans how to work!

"Our agents have reported nothing unusual. We have particularly close ties inside the American

Embassy in London. Reports indicate that the Americans were just as surprised as we were and, as of now, have no plans to take any action in their sector of Berlin."

"Keep the pressure on. We must be apprised of any verified instigation on their part as well as any planned actions. It is critical."

"Yes, Comrade. I will personally recheck all our sources," Chernoff replied trying not to appear to be condescending.

The rest of the meeting was a series of orders designed to regain control of the situation without bloodshed. It was clear that the resident chief and the division heads were also concerned about covering their collective asses from the wrath of Beria.

Not being a direct player in the action, Chernoff had time to absorb the situation. The Russians had failed miserably in their management of East Germany. Their puppet political party, the SED, the Socialist Unity Party, was a joke. The imposition of the communist concept on how to run the economy was a disaster. These debacles would not be so critical had not the prospering West Berlin sectors been so visible. The West Berliners were living better. Products from West Germany were superior to those being produced by the East Germans. The conclusion was obvious. The communist system just couldn't stand up against the capitalistic system under side-by-side comparison.

He wondered why these elite administrators couldn't see the inadequacies of their system and he began to feel uncomfortable. He had structured escape plans for each of his critical agents in case things went wrong. He had no such plan for himself. He snapped out of his reverie when Colonel Fadeikin pounded the table to emphasize a point. A recheck with his agents in London would be top on his list. He had two he knew he could count on.

* * *

"You're very early. We don't leave for another hour and a half," the purser of the ferry said as he looked at Parker's ticket.

"I'm on assignment for the National Geographic," Parker responded. "Just wanted to take a good look around for the best spots to take photographs before the boat got loaded."

"You're ticket is all the way to Alesund. We make a lot of stops with mail and cargo. If you want to get off at any spot, just keep your stub. We don't run every day so check the schedule. National Geographic? That's the one in yellow?"

"Yes."

"The Captain reads that one all the time. He's having a cup of coffee on the bridge," the Purser pointed. "Tell him I sent you. He'll be glad to have you as a passenger."

"Right up those stairs?" Parker feigned trying to establish a non-seafaring character.

"Go right up."

The Captain was looking over his chart as Parker approached. Borge Olson was not young. He was tall with gray hair, and his face was weathered by years of ocean spray. He was too old to fight in World War II. Somebody had to keep the ferries going, so Olson took it upon himself to be sure that the remote locations on the coast still had some access to the outside world. The Nazis made it difficult for him, so he took it upon himself to make things difficult for them. He personally did everything he could to hamper German shipping and supplies in and out of the Bergen harbor. The Nazis finally got the idea and began shipping supplies by rail from Oslo and left the harbor to the locals.

"Do you take pictures of animals in Africa? I'm always fascinated by how those shots are taken," Captain Olson said as he continued to study the chart.

"No, I stick to less adventuresome assignments. Mostly mountains, canyons, and things like that," Parker answered. He was getting to be an accomplished liar. Maybe this was one of the employee benefits of this assignment. "I have a map, but I'd appreciate any tips you have on any unusual sights along the way."

"This isn't a cruise ship, but I'll keep you in mind. Come up and we can talk some more when we are underway. Take a cup of coffee if you want." Captain Olson looked forward to some cargo being loaded.

Parker took the coffee. It was chilly at this hour of the morning. The North Sea is never warm, not even in June. He liked the feel of the ship. It brought back memories of good times on the destroyer and the companionship of the other officers. Since he came to London, he'd been too busy to reminisce. He also had no time to make real friends. The staff members at the Embassy were associates, not friends, and the mission contacts were brief and sterile. He longed for a personal, meaningful conversation. He hadn't spent more than an hour alone with Penelope and they were too busy with each other's body to talk. It had been a lonely two months.

The ferry slid from the pier flawlessly as a testament to Olson's seamanship. Parker selected a chair on the forward part of the first deck. He knew that the main deck would be covered by spray and wanted to get a good view of what was coming up. He opened his map and folded it so he could have Bergen northward in easy view to follow the passage. A small notebook was taken from the backpack. All he had to do was to wait.

* * *

Ivan brought in the morning mail and handed it to Chernoff. He grabbed the bundle from him.

"That will be all, Ivan," he barked. His knee ached and the pressure from the events in Berlin put him in a bad mood. Ivan was beginning to irritate him more than usual since he surmised that all of his moves were being reported to a higher level.

The weekly updates from the Russian Embassy in London and Paris had arrived. He scanned them hurriedly. Their reviews of the Berlin uprising were curt and almost identical. There was no evidence of British or American instigation. He would pass this information on to his superiors confirming his initial analyses.

The tension in Berlin persisted although the uprising was waning. Beria never made it to Berlin. He had been indicted in Moscow for crimes against the motherland. It was for a variety of incidents, but no mention of Berlin was made. While this took some pressure off the Berlin KGB chief, it did not bring closure to the matter. Certainly, Moscow would send someone to chop some heads.

Chernoff reflected as he stared out the window. They had only themselves to blame, yet he felt uneasy. The rumble of Russian tanks in the street below bothered him.

* * *

The distance between Bergen and Alesund is about 140 miles as the crow flies. The ferry route was a lot farther. The ship stopped at small villages not even noted on Parker's map and sometimes stopped at docks that appeared out of nowhere to deliver mail and pick up passengers. It would take the ship almost twenty hours to complete the trip, but since it was constant daylight at this latitude, it didn't matter. They would fuel and lay over a few hours at Alesund and begin the return run.

Parker had been carefully tracing the voyage on his map. Whenever he took a photo, he placed a number on the map. To keep his count right, every tenth photo he took a photo of a non-fjord item and copied the subject down in his logbook. So far nothing seemed to be close to what he was seeking,

"You read the chart well, Mr. Parkinson," Captain Olsen said as he dragged the cool North Sea air through his pipe. The ship seemed to be on a straight run north for awhile. "Steinborg is coming up port side. It is very isolated. We stop there only occasionally. Saevroy is starboard. They have the last good roads north from Bergen. Did you find anything interesting?"

"Not really," Parker answered. "I'm looking for something really steep, narrow, and not too long." Then he added, "Something the readers would not have seen before."

"We're going to be heading inland shortly to make a stop at Hardbakke." Olsen motioned Parker to come over to his chart. "This is also on an isolated island. Some of these may be just what you want." He circled with his finger an area on Parker's map. "You have the luxury of good weather, ideal for photography. We expect to have a high pressure area stall here for about a week."

Parker studied the contour of the island. A quick look up and down the chart showed that this was the only area where the fjords ran north south. This may be an advantage since the naval craft would be shaded except for a brief period around midday.

As they approached Hardbakke the island rose sharply. The fjords looked to be too wide, but Parker took some shots just for the record. The chart showed the northern side of the island to be uninhabited with narrower fjords. Parker wrapped up his chart. He had made his decision. When the ship came alongside the dock, Parker grabbed his backpack and photo bag and got off. He waved to the Captain.

"Good luck shooting," Captain Olsen shouted as he returned the wave

Parker quickly found a tavern. The National Geographic cover idea was excellent since everyone seemed to know the magazine. He made friends with the bar tender by taking his photograph and promising to get it into the magazine.

"So you need to get to the north side to take some pictures. First you must get to Krakhella on the east end of the island. There are no roads on the north side, so you need to hire a boat. Wait here a minute."

The bar keep swept around the bar to a table where four men were drinking and in a moment returned with a young man.

"I'm taking supplies from the ferry to Krakhella this afternoon. My name is Edvard. I hear you want a ride."

They quickly made a bargain. Parker paid the bar tab Edvard had been running for the past week in lieu of a fare.

The island was particularly rugged. Edvard drove the small truck over the narrow road at a racecar pace. There were no guardrails and Parker could look straight down from his seat on the passenger side. They did not slow down as they approached a small tunnel in the side of a cliff and it was only absence of other automobiles that saved them. It took them nearly an hour to reach Krakhella.

"There's only one boat in so far. You may want to talk to the captain." Edvard pointed out a small fishing craft with a lone man on board working on a net. "I think his name is Christian."

The boat was wooden and barely fifty feet long. Parker walked up and hailed the man.

"Did you get a good catch today?" Parker said in a loud voice to get his attention.

The man looked up and studied Parker. He turned towards the cabin and shouted something in

Norwegian. A head appeared. A figure came forward to where Parker was standing. Parker could see that it was a young girl in deck hand clothing, probably a teenager.

"Father say that you are Englishman. He do not speak much English."

The quality of her English told him that she had paid attention to her high school classes but probably didn't have an opportunity to practice. "I asked if he had a good catch today."

"Bad day. Trouble with net. We come in before other ships."

"I'm an American and I take photos for the National Geographic Magazine. I need to hire a boat for a few days to take me on the North side to photograph the fjords. Ask your father if he'd be interested."

"I know the magazine." She turned to her father. After a few minutes of conversation, she returned to the railing. "Father says $300 a day."

"Tell your father he has a deal."

She extended her hand to help him board the ship. Parker took a closer look. She was more mature than he had thought.

CHAPTER ELEVEN

Sven Christian loved his small fishing boat. He had followed in his father's footsteps and took over the fishing vessel upon his death. He refitted it for longer voyages and renamed it Nordstjernen, the North Star. A son would have been a big help, but he settled for a single daughter when the doctors informed his wife, Olga, she would not be able to conceive again. The young girl became a strong and helpful deck hand. Sven, Olga, and daughter, Ingrid, lived in a small house within comfortable walking distance of the wharf. The surrounding land was rock hard and steep except for a garden in a small plot next to the house. It appeared to be the only tillable soil within view.

Parker was invited to share dinner. When Olga appeared with the platter of fish he was not surprised. As Ingrid interpreted, her English was becoming better.

"Father say you can stay on board the Star. We do not have room here. There are blankets to keep you warm. Expect to get an early start. We take all day to look around on the North side"

"Sounds good to me."

"It may be a little rough. Do you like boats?"

"It doesn't bother me. I hear the weather should be good for the next week, so we should not have any trouble. I want to take a lot of pictures. I'd guess we'd need at least three days to do what I want."

The family talked in Norwegian. Parker finished his fish. He couldn't tell what kind of fish it was but it tasted good. Olga seemed to be pleased that Parker enjoyed the meal.

"Mother wants to know if you have been working for National Geographic a long time. You are very young."

"Less than two years," Parker shaded the truth with remarkable ease. "My camera is used for long shots, but tell your mother that I will take some photos of the family and send them to you."

Ingrid relayed the message and Olga smiled. Swen just nodded that he understood.

"I walk with you back to the boat and see you get settled. There is a small alcohol stove for heating water. You'll want to make tea. I'll bring some of mother's bakery for breakfast. It should be a good day."

"Are you coming along for the trip?"

"Of course, maybe I learn to be a photographer."

Walking to the boat, Parker struggled to not watch the comely young woman at his side.

He knew he needed to keep focused and carefully act out his part tomorrow if only to protect the reputation of the National Geographic Society.

"Father says the next fjord is coming up. I explain that you need to take other photos. Take some of him."

Parker made another mark on the map and pointed at the new fjord. Sven nodded. This one looked even better than the first.

The day was crystal clear and perfect for photography. They were making good time and both the men concentrated on marking the map making sure the film roll and frame numbers tracked. Parker made copious notes in his log. At noon, Ingrid interrupted them with a lunch that Olga had provided.

Parker and Ingrid sat on the deck and began their lunch while Christian brought the North Star into the wind and slowed the engines to a crawl.

"It's a beautiful day," Ingrid said as she gazed towards the horizon.

"It's good to be here with such a beautiful companion," Parker countered.

"Jimmy, it is very lonely here," she said thoughtfully. "You see a lot of different things and people all the time, don't you?"

"The job takes me a lot of different places, but I don't get to know many people. I move around too much."

"Where do you go from here?"

"Alesund. I expect to have some spare time so I want to spend a few days there, then take the fast ferry to Trondheim. I've got a flight back to London in about ten days." Parker began to eat a cheese sandwich.

"You might need a guide and an interpreter. Not too many people talk English as you go north." Ingrid turned and looked at Parker. She poured some tea for both of them.

"I like you, Jimmy," she said looking into his eyes. "Father likes you, too. He told me so."

"You are the nicest person I've met during my travels for National Geographic." Parker smiled. At least this was not a lie.

By the end of the day Parker was sure that he had a good view of the north side of the island. After they docked, he offered to take them to dinner at the tavern in town. They accepted. He returned early to the boat to complete his notes. The lighting in the wheelhouse was poor, so he went below to the small cabin where the light was better. There he was able to check his map against the logbook and carefully review how many pictures he had taken. The silence broken only by waves lapping at the sides of the boat helped his concentration. He was carefully making a plan for tomorrow's run to take close up shots of particular fjords when he heard footsteps on the deck.

Parker quickly folded his notebook. His alert system snapped into gear. No one could have followed him here to this desolate spot in Norway, but he couldn't take chances. He flicked the light off reaching back to grip his revolver as he backed against the cabin bulkhead; his pulse rate doubled.

The door to the cabin slowly opened and Parker began to draw his pistol. Ingrid's golden hair was framed by the doorway. Parker let out a breath and released his grip on the gun

"Are you there, Jimmy?"

Parker snapped the light on. "I was just heading up to the wheelhouse."

"Mother sent this desert for you, Jimmy. She thought you may not have enough food at the tavern." Ingrid moved to the small alcohol stove and lit the wick under the teapot. "The tea will be ready in a moment." She sat down at the small table and waited for Parker to join her.

"Jimmy, tell me something about your travels. I have not traveled past Bergen. Have you been to New York?"

Parker could sense her frustration at the isolation of the island. "Yes, I've been to New York. It's a lot bigger than Bergen. You wouldn't like it."

Ingrid laughed. They talked. And they talked. It did both of them good. For Ingrid, Parker was a window to the world she longed to explore. For Parker, Ingrid was someone who listened.

"Your Father is going to be worried." Parker grabbed her hand and made her rise. Ingrid came closer and kissed him. Parker spun her around and gave her a swat on her rear. "Get going!"

As she left the ship, Parker looked at his hand. Ingrid was firm, but not hard. He wondered what the age of consent was in Norway.

The next two days, the North Star made trips into each of the fjords Parker had targeted. Sven showed great seamanship in maneuvering in and out. Even Ingrid got caught up in the charting. She had keen eyes and pointed out many things that would have slipped by Parker. Her English was rapidly becoming fluent. Parker told them that he would be moving out the next day and asked Ingrid to arrange for someone to take him to Hardbakke where he could catch the ferry to Alesund. The Christians invited Parker for dinner the last evening. He counted out 12 one hundred-dollar bills on the table and thanked him for his work.

"I told Father you asked me to be your guide and interpreter for the next week," Ingrid said at what she thought was the proper time.

Parker's jaw dropped in astonishment. "You what?"

"He said that you probably would need the help."

Parker turned towards Sven.

"It is OK," Sven said in almost perfect English. "You will be good for her."

The stay in Alesund was a relief for Parker. He didn't realize the stress he was under until he started to relax. The weather stayed good as predicted. Ingrid was right about the English being less often spoken as you went north. She turned out to be the perfect guide as well as the perfect companion. She was smart and observant. On their first night at the hotel, Ingrid was quick to spot the revolver. "What is the gun for, Jimmy? Are you expecting trouble?"

"Just a precaution when I'm traveling," Parker responded. "I always carry a lot of cash. Don't touch it. There is no safety."

Ingrid didn't believe that story at all, but didn't pursue the subject. She had other things on her mind. Somewhere she had learned the art of massage and applied it well. They might not be falling in love with each other, but they were falling in love with each other's body. Ingrid's skin was smooth and taut while the flesh beneath showed the resilience of youth and hard work. In bed she would wrap her legs around him to lock him into position, then rhythmically release him. They rolled and wrestled in passion until they climaxed, then they would start again.

Parker kept his camera bag with the exposed film at his side at all times. He didn't feel threatened, but occasionally he suspected that someone was following them. They took hikes in the mountains and toured the surrounding areas when not relaxing at the hotel. He took photographs of the countryside to keep busy and to maintain his cover

His two-week time limit was nearly up. He booked his open return flight from Trondheim-Bergen-London from the hotel.

"I want to come with you to Trondheim, Jimmy. Take me to Trondheim, I can get back from there," Ingrid pleaded. They stood in front of the southbound ferry ready to depart.

"I promised your father that I'd put you on the ferry back to Hardbakke. No sense you going to Trondheim. I'm taking the fast ship and then go right to the airport."

Ingrid cried. "I'm never going to see you again, Jimmy. I'm going to end up on that island working on the North Star the rest of my life." She sobbed and tears streamed down her face. "How could you do this to me?"

James held her close and kissed her. "Ingrid, you're a bright, beautiful young lady. You won't need me to find a way out of Krakhella."

The boat pulled away. Ingrid stood on the stern waving. Parker felt sad and alone. He didn't realize how much he had grown to care for Ingrid until the small figure on the ship began to be blurred by the sea mist. He then turned. He had a job to do.

The coastal steamer was larger than the ferry and much faster. Parker was sure he could make the late flight from Trondheim to Bergen and still catch the last flight to London. The sky was cloudy. A cold front was moving in and the fine weather Parker had enjoyed was coming to an end. In what had become a habit, he found a convenient spot on the ship and set up his camera. He elected the starboard side so he could shoot the coastline.

The weather front came in quicker than he had expected. The rain started as Parker had just begun photographing. He moved amid ship so he was somewhat shielded from the storm. The passengers quickly sought shelter inside with the exception of one man who was standing alone in the rain near the stern of the ship. When the deck was cleared of passengers, he started to move towards Parker.

It was getting too dark for photographs. Parker decided to put his camera away in the bag when he noticed the man and wondered why he wasn't inside like the rest of the passengers. At about ten feet away, he caught sight of the automatic pistol in the stranger's hand.

"Pick up the bag slowly and drop it over the side" Antoine said with authority enforced by the pistol. He had been instructed by Chernoff to intercept Parker and interfere with the mission, but not to take him out. Parker might be useful to them later. Antoine looked with disdain at the neophyte. His years working for the Russians all over Europe made this mission seem like a vacation.

Parker's whole body tightened. He recognized the Frenchman he had seen in Rome and Copenhagen. The rain started coming down in sheets and the wind started to pick up. Lightning could be seen in the sky.

"Now, slowly, *lentement.* I don't want to kill you." Antoine wanted to get out of the cold rain pelting him.

He knew making Parker drop the bag overboard would mess up his mission, whatever it was.

Parker was trapped. He finished placing the camera in the bag, then picked it up slowly with his left hand turning his body so that the Frenchman could not see his right hand moving to his back searching for the revolver. He was certain the Frenchman was going to kill him. If he lost the film, he might as well be killed anyway. He found the gun just as his left hand had the bag at the height of the railing. With a single motion, he dropped the bag, pulled the gun out and fired as he ducked.

The Frenchman was caught totally by surprise. He jumped backwards, feeling the bullet piercing his right shoulder. He was off balance but he fired his automatic as if by a reflex action. Parker fired two more shots which missed their mark, but they caused the Frenchman to scamper for cover on the rain sheathed steel deck. He slipped just as a swell caught the ship and slid feet first through the rail opening near the scupper. Parker rushed to the rail still holding the gun and looked down. The Frenchman had disappeared. A crewmember appeared from a hatchway. Parker effortlessly released the pistol which fell into the sea, then turned around.

"Man overboard!" Parker shouted and grabbed the sailor. "Man overboard!" He pointed quickly over to the side.

The sailor looked then ran forward and waved frantically. The helmsman recognized his signal and gave three short blasts on the ship's horn and turned the ship hard to port then hard starboard, making the standard man overboard maneuver.

Captain Erickson immediately radioed nearby Kristiansund for assistance. He would need all the help he could get as the rain was rapidly reducing visibility. He began a crossing pattern to search the area as best he could. He moved towards his second in command. "Have the sailor who reported the incident come to the bridge. Also get any witnesses."

It was fifteen minutes before Parker and the sailor came to the bridge. There was a brief conversation in Norwegian as the sailor told his story. The Captain then turned to Parker.

"I need some information for my report. Did you see what happened?"

"Everyone was coming in from the rain. I was putting my camera equipment away when I saw this man coming forward on the deck. The lightning and thunder must have startled him and he started to run. He lost his balance as the ship rolled and slipped through the bottom of the railing. When I looked down, he was gone."

"Did you know him?"

"No."

"Can you give us a description?"

"It was raining very hard. I couldn't see his face."

"The deckhand said he heard shots and was coming to investigate. Did he have a gun?"

"No, I didn't see a gun. But there was thunder."

"I need your passport identification for the report."

Parker gave him his ID from National Geographic as well.

"On assignment with National Geographic?"

"Yes. I'm doing a spread on the fjords north of Bergen."

The government ship from Kristiansund had arrived on the scene. There was a flurry of communications back and forth between the two vessels. The captain then ordered the helmsman to resume course north.

"They've released us but will continue the search by themselves. I will radio the information into the Ministry of Coastal Affairs in Trondheim. I'll have to ask you to stay aboard in case they need any further information. We seldom lose anyone at this time of the year so they will consider this very unusual."

"What are the chances of rescuing that man?" Parker asked.

"Little to none. The North Sea is cold and the bodies sink quickly. The fish usually finish off the body before it has a chance to rise."

Parker was surprisingly calm. His breathing was steady and he was able to look straight at the Captain. He felt no remorse for the Frenchman. He got rid of the gun as Higgins had directed as if by post-hypnotic suggestion. This wasn't like his first mission in Munich. He couldn't define his feelings now, but whatever they were he knew he didn't like them.

The corkboards in Evans' office were covered with photographs. The good weather made the photos clear and sharp. The numbers written on each exposure referred to the sketch Parker had made of the fjords. A large detailed map of the Norwegian coastline hung on the adjacent wall.

"Your sketch is a good match for the map, Parker. You didn't major in art, did you?"

Smythe commented as he examined the photos with a magnifying glass.

"Just mechanical drawing," Parker countered as they huddled around the photos. "I thought these were the best slots for destroyers," he added as he pointed to two photos. "Just far enough to have the destroyers complement each other in air defense, and forcing the planes to choose a single target."

"The plan is to hide the ships. Live firing defense would be secondary." Foxworthy butted in.

"I'd back the destroyers into the fjords. There's not enough room to turn around comfortably, particularly if there is any action." Parker felt proud of himself. The photos turned out better than he expected. His tenth shots were posted off to the side and almost created a travelogue. The photos of Christian and his boat were Geographic quality. The photos of Ingrid were striking. Parker started to feel bad about leaving her. Evans broke the spell.

"We have enough information here to complete a plan," Evans said with a nodding head motion towards Foxworthy. He then turned towards Parker and changed his tone to accusatory. "You were two days behind schedule. We don't expect our operatives to be late. Higgins reported your gun is missing." He motioned for everyone to take a seat then added sarcastically, "We'd all like to hear your explanation."

Parker told of the episode aboard the coastal steamer. He had been detained in Trondheim until they were able to check out his identification. "Someone must have done a good job of providing the cover. The National Geographic was very complimentary of my work. Maybe I can get a job with them when I get out."

Evans did not appreciate the humor. "Are you positive this was the Frenchman you saw in Rome and in Copenhagen? Could it have been just a random robbery?"

"No doubt whatsoever," Parker emphatically responded. "Beside the accent, he used a French word. He wasn't interested in stealing the camera. He distinctly ordered me to throw the camera bag containing the film overboard. He was messing with my brain. What I can't figure out is how he found me."

"Did you tell anyone you were going to Norway?"

"No one, not even Chad. I made sure that nobody was following me after I left his flat. I took so many metros that even I was getting confused."

"Your assailant could have been a Russian agent. If it was, you are going to be very unpopular in Moscow."

Smythe interrupted what was becoming an awkward situation. "Parker, there aren't any assignments pending right now so if Conrad doesn't need you in coding, take a few days off while we digest this material."

Parker got permission to leave. He headed straight toward Selfridges.

CHAPTER TWELVE

Airy wasn't difficult to find. The Administration Department of Selfridges was very helpful directing him to the High Fashion Women's Dress section on the 8th floor. He thanked the clerk and took the elevator.

She was looking over a display that had a mannequin in an evening gown holding a champagne glass. Parker moved in close behind her.

"Could you direct me to the men's clothing section?"

Airy spun around. A surprised look gave way to a smile.

"Damn, I used that line before, didn't I?" Parker quipped.

Airy burst out laughing. It was the kind of laugh that Parker liked.

"You did find me! Well, I'm flattered. Did your trip go well?

"As well as could be expected. Right now I've got my mind set on dinner. Do you have any plans?"

"There's a fine Chinese restaurant in the Kensington area close to my place. Are you interested?

"Some of my best friends are Chinese."

"I'll jot down my address and you can come around to my flat at about six. That will give me a chance to freshen up. You're Bob Smith, aren't you?" Airy taunted with a smile waiting for a reaction then added, "No, it's Parker, James Parker isn't it?"

Parker retorted, "You can call me Bob if you want to."

The game was over. Both were smiling. Airy wrote out her address.

Parker rang the flat. "Lieutenant Parker to see Miss Reynolds."

"I'll be right down."

Even in casual clothes, Airy looked stunning to James. Her father was English-Irish, but her mother was Irish through and through. Her heritage showed throughout her body and persona. The war had bypassed them in Northern Ireland. Dad had a critical job in a factory and the Germans never seemed to get that far North with their bombing. Besides, the neighboring Irish Free State was neutral and Hitler didn't want to risk pulling them into the war. He had his hands full with the English and the United States.

After the war, the Irish economy went into a tailspin and the recession spilled over into Northern Ireland as well. Work for men was particularly scarce and a seamstress job in a garment factory was considered almost a royal appointment. When Airy finished high school she was fortunate to get a job as a clerk in a department store in Londonderry. Her flair for style showed up in display work. Quick wit and good looks gained her occasional modeling assignments. Even in the best of times, she barely made enough to cover food and clothing and therefore continued to live with her parents.

At the age of 21, Harriet Reynolds decided it was time to go to London to seek her fortune. Building on her experience in Londonderry, she was able to land a job as a clerk at Selfridges. When a position as an assistant buyer opened up she applied for it. Her ability to model the clothes she selected was a definite plus. She liked her work and worked hard, determined to leave the poverty of Northern Ireland behind her forever. She only occasionally dated. She didn't want to get involved while still working her way to financial stability. What made her rash enough to tell a near stranger that she would have dinner with him, she couldn't figure out. Maybe it was the uniform.

To Parker, Airy was some gorgeous thing delivered to him by chance. Their conversation progressed well beyond the sweet sour sauce and chopsticks as they mentally explored each other.

"So you've really not had a job other than the Navy."

"You might say that, but I definitely don't plan on making the Navy my career. I may want to get into teaching."

"What would you teach?"

"Math, I think. I should be eligible to get a masters degree with the benefits from this tour of duty. Maybe I could get a job teaching at a small college."

"You might do well. You seem to have a way with people." Airy was beginning to relax The green tea was warm and aromatic. She sensed a good feeling.

"What about you, Airy? I don't see you retiring from Selfridges as chief buyer."

"Right now I'm just pleased to be a buyer. I can pay my bills on time and send a few pounds home to Mom and Dad."

On the way back to the flat, they held hands as they ran across the street dodging the traffic. It was as if electricity passed between them. Neither one could ever remember feeling anything like that before.

"Forgive me for not asking you up. The flat's a mess and I have a heavy day tomorrow. Do you dance?"

"They call me Cleveland's answer to Fred Astaire."

"Good. There's a dance just few blocks away on Saturday night. I'd like to show you off to some of my friends."

"I'm your slave," Parker answered with a bow.

For the next few days Parker had no new courier assignments. Work in the coding room was boring until Thursday morning, July 23, when it seemed that every teletype machine began clicking at the same time. Coded messages were coming in, but it was the clear language message that told it all. An armistice was signed ending hostilities in the Korean War.

Captain Foxworthy's office was jammed with Navy and Marine personnel. He finished reading the decoded messages, then called a meeting of all personnel reporting to himself or Smythe. When he stood up behind his desk, the room became quiet.

"You all know the good news. The armistice in Korea has been signed. However, the field commanders have been informed that there will be no change in allocation of resources or repositioning of troops in the immediate future. The United States wants to make sure that nothing is done that the Chinese could interpret as weakness. There is to be no change in alert status anywhere without specific instructions from Washington. For us this means business as usual. Any questions?"

"Any input on the Russian reaction?" a senior Marine officer asked.

"It's too early to have received any reports. The Russians are just getting the Berlin situation under control. There is some feeling that they may make some desperation move before we can reallocate our forces, but I personally doubt it. Those of you in the intelligence operations should be particularly alert for any attitude changes."

Parker raised his hand. "Any change in reserve status, sir?"

"No. It's usually six months after cessation of hostilities before the reserves are cut back. If there are no other questions, you are dismissed."

That Saturday Airy took particular pleasure showing Parker off to her dance hall friends. It was a dress up affair and she asked him to wear his uniform. The couple stood out in the crowd. Both appeared as if they had been dancing together for years as their bodies melted together on the dance floor. Parker picked up the quick step and in turn gave Airy some pointers on the Lindy.

During the next week they spent every evening together. Hours were spent getting to know each other. They kissed passionately and often. They were falling in love. Airy drew the line just at the bedroom door. James didn't want to rush things, but he was having trouble reconciling a relationship of love without sex. Airy wasn't having any trouble with it.

"Strict Protestant religious upbringing frowns upon pre-marital sex," Airy said unconvincingly. She was seated lengthwise on the couch leaning across James' lap looking upward. He brought her closer to him and pressed his lips upon hers, then leaned back.

"I thought that was only for the Irish Catholics."

"No. The Catholics talk a good story but seem to have no problem with sex. Maybe it's because they can go to confession and get forgiven the next day. It's not that easy for the Protestants. They have to wrestle with their own consciences." She kissed Parker throwing her arms around him, bending him over. "Seriously, James, a physical relationship with a sailor doesn't exactly represent the kind of stability of which my parents would approve."

"Airy, I'm not going to be in the Navy forever. The Korean War is over and I should be released soon."

"You know I can't help loving you, but I do need some time."

"How about 15 minutes?"

She gave him a peck kiss. "How about behaving yourself for a few days. I'm going to visit Mom and Dad over the weekend. Stay away from those girls at the Embassy."

Parker toyed with her breast. "I don't know if I can wait that long." He ran his tongue deep into her mouth. Her body molded to his. Her body was ready even if her mind wasn't.

If CIA Station Chief Evans was relieved that the Korean situation was stabilized, he didn't show it. There were four lead pencils on his desk showing a multitude of teeth marks, a habit from high school that he couldn't seem to shake. Smythe and Parker were seated across the desk from him. He spoke rapidly and directly to Parker.

"We have an interest in a small book distributor in London specializing in nonfiction American books. You will be their sales representative for Copenhagen," Evans instructed without changing the tone of his voice. "Next week you will begin a simple routine. Every Thursday you will fly to Copenhagen, stay overnight and return the next morning. You will still have the first part of the week free to make runs to the various embassies."

"That should leave weekends on my own," said Parker making mental notes in a date book with Airy's name underlined.

Without responding, Evans continued. "Using this sales rep cover, you will take copies of new releases to the Copenhagen stores encouraging the proprietors to review them. There are only three stores on your list, all near the center of Copenhagen. You will pick up any books that haven't sold. There will always be at least one book to be brought back. You will be wearing civilian clothes, obviously, and you will carry an automatic weapon for your personal safety. It is important that you make these trips look as routine as possible. Don't make this complicated. Any questions?"

"Never thought I'd be in the book business," Parker stated. He had learned there was no chance of asking a question which would receive an answer.

"You will do a reasonable amount of entertaining of the store managers. Spend at least half your evenings at the Tivoli Gardens."

"I think I can handle that."

"Take the usual precautions. Continue to operate out of Conrad's flat. He's been told that you have a weekly departure beginning next Thursday."

Smythe put his coffee down and changed position in his chair. "We do have a courier assignment to fill in your time over this weekend. From your Norwegian photos we have selected certain locations for refuge in case of Russian aggression. These will be part of the order of battle for all ships departing the U. S. to the area. The two destroyers and a submarine currently operating in the North Sea pose a different problem. We don't want to take the chance that they won't have a current plan of battle if things get hot suddenly. The plan needs to be hand delivered at once."

"I'm glad you found my photography work useful."

"The destroyers pull into Inverness Scotland this weekend for recreational shore leave. We'll provide transportation to get you there. You'll be in uniform with a pouch. The submarine is a little more complicated. It's on station north of Ireland doing classified surveillance and has no port of call. Ever been to Ireland?" Smythe opened a map on the office table.

"No I haven't. Ireland isn't part of NATO," Parker pointed out almost in the form of a question. "They've been neutral since they broke away from England in 1922."

"The history lesson is not necessary, Lieutenant. Obviously, handling the sub is a delicate situation. Because its mission is classified, CINCLANT doesn't want it pulling into any port. The sub is going to send a party ashore to pick up the pouch. The only good spot on Ireland's northern side is a small town called Buncrana. It's sheltered and the shores slope gently. A contact from the sub will meet you Sunday at a prearranged time and place. You will be staying at a hotel in Londonderry in Northern Ireland. The cross to Ireland will be in civilian clothes. You should have no problem since there is always a heavy flow of civilians. The Protestants close everything down on Sunday in Londonderry but the wild ones cross over to Buncrana for the day for beer and to taunt the Catholics. The Catholics put up with it to get the hard English currency. Be sure you blend into the crowd. Don't drink too much, stay out of politics, and you should have no problems."

"Will there be anything to pick up from the ships?"

"No, why do you ask?"

"Well, if I don't have to carry back any classified material, I may want to stay over in Londonderry to do some sight seeing before I start the Denmark run. Would that be possible?"

Smythe gave a quick glance at Evans. Evans nodded. "All right, but stay out of trouble."

Evans looked up with a dead serious expression. "The Copenhagen mission to establish a routine is of the utmost importance and we want it to go smoothly. You must be back here from Londonderry by 0800 Wednesday morning so we can prepare you to leave Thursday according to plan.

"Yes, sir." Parker couldn't wait to tell the good news to Airy.

"I can't believe it. You're going to be in Londonderry the same weekend as I am? Doesn't that sound a bit weird?" Airy asked.

"You can imagine how I felt when I was told to report there. It was a struggle for me to keep a straight face. As for being weird, my whole life has been like this."

"What could you possibly be doing in Derry?"

"Airy, it's just Navy business, but it's all very serious stuff and you don't want to get involved." Parker paused and smiled. Airy returned the smile. "It's perfectly routine." Parker was getting to talk more like Smythe every day.

"Well, my folks will be surprised."

"I'll be at the Trinity Hotel. Ask them to dinner Saturday night. I may have only the one night in town. I'm anxious to get to know them."

"You'll get to know each other all right," she replied in a mocking tone. Airy wasn't prepared to have the meeting so soon. Both parents were very protective of their only child and didn't approve of her expedition to London. It would be hard to make them believe that James was just a friend. "Better to have you over to dinner. It will be on their home ground. Besides, you ought to see how the Irish live."

The two destroyers, the Harris and the Pitman, were just coming into view through the early morning mist as Parker stood on the wharf in Inverness. The approach on the Moray Firth was tricky and the ships appeared to be taking their time. The wharf was crowded with dignitaries and port officials. The visit of two United States Naval vessels was important to the economy and the townspeople were determined to make them feel welcome. Parker estimated there were at least 50 young women, most of whom were carrying bouquets of heather. It looked like the first liberty party was going to have the best pickings.

The Harris docked inboard indicating the seniority of Captain Morrison. He was not any more friendly than when they met in Bordeaux.

"Still playing the messenger boy, Lieutenant?" Morrison taunted as he signed the receipt documents in the wardroom.

"It's a rotten job, sir, but somebody's got to do it." Parker wasn't about to back down this time.

Captain Morrison looked up. "We received the coded message that you would be making an important delivery to both ships and would be briefing us on the contents. I have asked Captain of the Pitman to come to the wardroom as soon as his ship is secured. Sit down and relax." Morrison motioned to the Stewards Mate to set up coffee. "What's going on in London, Parker? I've been on station out here for almost twelve weeks and they don't tell us doodlie squat."

Parker sipped his coffee. "Well, they crowned a queen. I have seen the television clips of the truce signed in Korea, so it must be true. They don't tell me much on purpose."

Captain Morrison began to fire another question when there was a knock and a much younger Lt. Commander entered. He was so tall that he had to bend over to get through the hatch.

"Lt. Parker, Captain Landis. His ship will replace mine next week."

They shook hands. Parker spoke. "I have to get right to the subject. My plane is waiting just outside Inverness. I've got another stop and I'd like to get there while it is still daylight."

Morrison nodded acquiescence and opened the pouch and handed the contents to Parker. He spread the map on the table.

"This map gives details of the coast of Norway." The three leaned over the table to get a better look as Parker reviewed the plan of battle with particular attention to the fjords to be used as a refuge. "Now that things have reached a status quo in Korea, we've been promised three destroyers on station in the North Sea." Looking at Captain Morrison, he continued. "Just when the other two cans will be freed up has not been determined."

The two captains continued to look over the map. They exchanged a few comments between them, and then Landis turned toward Parker. "I think I've got a good fix on this."

Parker handed the duplicate pouch to him. "I'll need both your signatures on the receipt."

Landis was much younger than Morrison and in considerably better physical shape. His stripes glistened proclaiming a recent promotion. Parker could see the changing of the guard from the weather beaten faces of World War II to the freshly scrubbed, recent Academy graduates who had just missed combat.

"Too bad you're in a hurry. They say this is a fine liberty port for our plebes and crew," Landis commented.

Morrison interrupted. He couldn't contain himself. "Damnit, Parker, you know what's going on! They wouldn't send you out here on a special plane if they weren't expecting something and something soon."

"I've told you all I know, sir." It suddenly dawned on Parker what the problem was. The old sea dog was itching for just one more battle before he headed for shore duty and retirement. He knew he had just one more week at sea and it would be all over for him.

Morrison continued to badger. "You say you've got another stop. There are other U.S. ships in this area, aren't there? They're planning something, aren't they?"

"All I can say is the next stop is classified."

Morrison lost it. "You're fucking worthless, Parker."

Parker methodically gathered up his remaining pouch. He rose to depart. "I'm not so sure about that, sir." He had no intention of asking permission to leave.

On the dock a comely young lass grabbed Parker's arm as he walked to his waiting car. She had a snap in her step and the glint of Scotland in her eye. "You've got a very big gun there, Commander," she said as she pointed to his holster. "You're not leaving us, are you?"

Parker loved these instant promotions. He stopped, grabbed the girl. and spun her around close into him. "If you behave yourself, I'll come back for you."

She sighed, "Then there's no use you coming back."

She was probably right.

To say the Reynolds home was small and simple would have been generous. Parker felt uneasy in his well tailored civilian clothes. Their clothes were commonplace and wrinkled. Airy's parents were definitely looking him over. He made sure to compliment Katie Reynolds on the meal. The conversation was courteous, but bordered on formality. Airy's father was curious about the small pouch that Parker kept with him, but not to the point of being obnoxious.

"James expects to be out of the Navy soon now that the Koreans have signed a truce. He's a mathematics professor," Airy pointed out trying to bolster her beau.

"Does teaching pay well?" Michael Reynolds asked.

"It's a living. You probably won't get rich, but it's what I want to do," he said picking up Airy's cue.

It was not the answer the senior Reynolds was looking for. His daughter should be looking for a man with position and money. He wanted to trust his daughter's judgment, but couldn't leave her out of the nest right now.

Airy felt disappointment might be clouding the air. "I'm going to take James for a walk around town and then to the cinema. We won't be out late."

Airy suggested they walk to the hotel. She had only seen the inside of the Trinity hotel once. "Show me around, Jimmy. We've got time before we have to queue up for the cinema."

They stopped in the bar for a quick drink. "I think they like you, Jimmy."

"I hope so although it was hard to tell. Your father couldn't take his eyes off that pouch. I wanted to tell him it was just penicillin for the sailors, but I'm not allowed to breach security."

"That's not funny, James."

"Relax, Airy. Come on up to the room for a minute. I need to check for messages. You've got to see how I'm spending the United States dollar."

Parker had the best room in the hotel. It was a suite with a sitting room, bedroom and a bath.

"I'm impressed, Jimmy."

"Nothing but first class when you're on government business."

Airy began shyly, "Mother said she knows I'm having sex with you. She told me to be careful."

"Hmmmmm."

Airy walked to the door, locked it, and turned towards Parker. She slowly walked towards him. "Mother's always been right."

The dam had been broken for Airy and her sexuality flowed out filling the room as she slowly began to undress. The redness of the nipples on her breasts emphasized by the whiteness of her skin was startling. Parker drew her gently to the bed and turned off the bedroom light plunging the room into darkness. He had seen enough.

There was no movie for them that evening.

Parker left the Trinity Hotel in time to catch the 1100 bus to Buncrana. His suitcase containing his uniform remained at the hotel where he could return for them on his trip back to London. Airy had pleaded with Parker to take her with him. She had been to Buncrana many times and she could be helpful. Parker would have none of it. He had gotten her home last night just early enough for her parents not to be suspicious

He felt out of place on the bus. His clothes weren't right and his shoulder holster was a little too bulgy. The pouch was too different from the packages others were carrying. It drew glances from the passengers. The ride took only about 40 minutes and there was no border stop. Evidently the buses from Derry on Sunday carrying hard cash were more than welcome.

The town was small. The passengers on the bus were greeted with two men wildly flailing their arms at each other in the middle of the square. They were too inebriated to do any real damage to each other, but the crowd had gathered to urge them on just for the hell of it.

Parker inquired from an onlooker for the whereabouts of O'Flaherty's Tavern. A man pointed down the street without taking his eyes off the fight.

Parker entered the tavern early. He felt that he had a better chance of blending into the bar crowd than out front in the street. Blending turned out to be not that easy. Off the lobby was a huge taproom. The locals and the tourists from Derry had turned the air blue with cigarette smoke and the patrons were beginning to feel the beer even though it was barely noon. The tables were nearly all filled with characters out of Dickens. He grabbed a stool at the bar to take a look around.

In his college days, Parker always had bad luck at bars. He could be seated minding his own business and ask someone to pass the salt and the next thing you know, he'd be in a fight.

"I'll have a beer," Parker raised his voice to the bar tender.

"Comin' "

The man to his left turned around. "You're nae from around here, now are you, son?"

"No, I just came over from Derry. Nothing going on over there on a Sunday and my thirst got the better of me."

The man leaned closer. He smelled of ale. "You're not Derry Irish, are you?" he asked as menacingly even though he could barely maintain his balance.

"No."

A man to Parker's right laid a heavy hand on Parker's right shoulder. Parker turned. The man who was definitely not sober asked, "Then you're Catholic, are ya?"

"I'm an American. I just came to have a beer," Parker answered trying to avoid being drawn in. Regardless, he was attracting the kind of attention he didn't want. Two men who were passing by towards the end of the bar stopped and took notice. Parker had his back to the bar. He couldn't determine whose side these guys were on.

The drunk got closer than he wanted. "What's in the bag, Sonny, your lunch? Maybe you'd like to share it with us."

Shit! Parker thought. Just my luck to have to shoot someone in the Irish Free State to protect NATO documents. He wasn't ready to panic yet, but this was getting close to being one of Higgins' "you'll know" situations.

A tap on the shoulder came from across the bar. "Here's your beer, Lad," the bartender said breaking the suspense. Parker turned around. He grabbed his wallet quickly as he felt that a crowd was beginning to gather around him.

"I want to buy a drink for everyone at the bar," Parker told the barkeep. "See how far this goes." He laid a fifty-dollar bill on the bar.

The bartender grabbed the money and raised it above his head and announced, "This gentlemen is buying beer for everyone at the bar."

The rush towards the bar was like a tidal wave, sweeping away his potential adversaries. Parker held his pouch firmly and ducked through the on-coming hordes. He retreated toward the entrance observing the near riot he had created. Only a few of the more reserved souls remained at their tables.

"DiMaggio."

Parker turned towards the voice. He was a young man wearing a black leather jacket and a black knit hat. It was his contact.

"56", Parker responded.

"That was some performance you put on there. I thought for a moment you were going to end up right in the middle of the Irish civil war," the man said. "I'm Lt. Anderson, XO of the Bluefish. I've got some friends at a table over in that corner. We've got time for a drink now that everyone else is distracted."

"Lt. Parker. With the London Embassy," Parker said extending his hand. "Did you have any trouble making it ashore?"

"No, this is more or less a routine stop for us. It's not really R and R, but if we need a Band-Aid or something, we are always able to get it in this town."

"Sounds a bit risky."

"Not really."

Andrews introduced two other men dressed in similar garb as enlisted crewmembers.

Parker declined an offer to have a beer. The bar was still in turmoil.

"Where's the sub?"

"We don't tie up, you know." Andrews said smiling. "We just drop off a detail in an inflatable landing raft and then go out far enough to submerge until the pickup time. In the summer, the weather is good enough so there is no problem."

"Unbelievable."

"Probably not any more risky than what you are doing. Besides, this is a historic meeting place for naval vessels. During the war, the German subs would drop off landing parties for supplies and the British frigates would also come in to have a beer. It was a neutral port. Legend has it that they would share a drink together one day then go back to hunting each other the next."

"That's got to be one hell of a war story."

"Take a look over there." Andrews pointed to a table in the other corner of the room. There were four men dressed not unlike the Americans he was sitting with. It was obvious that they were definitely not townspeople. "Those are Russian submariners. They come in about once every two weeks to replenish their vodka supply."

Parker didn't know whether or not to believe him. He strained to get a better look. "Have you ever spoken to them?"

"No. I hear that the Russian movies are terrible, otherwise we'd try to exchange flicks," Anderson joked.

It was time to get down to business. "I need your signature. The pouch contains a plan for a hiding spot for destroyers and submarines in case you get in a sticky situation. The maps and photos contain sufficient information to get by on. I'd like to point out a few more things, but obviously we can't spread the map out here. If you have any luck at all, the Russians won't make any moves while you are on station here. Replacement ships will be briefed in more detail before they depart from the States."

Andrews signed the receipt and took possession of the pouch. "We'll finish our beer and be on our way. You'd better leave first since you were the center of attention. We'll follow shortly and cover your ass in case there is any more trouble."

"Thanks. By the way, it was the Cleveland Indians who ended DiMaggio's streak at 56."

"It was really third baseman Kenny Keltner. We Yankee fans still call him the biggest thief since Jesse James."

CHAPTER THIRTEEN

KGB Station Chief at the Paris Embassy, Rimski Clovich, sat frozen at his desk. His career at this choice Paris location was on the line. Boris Chernoff, his superior who had just flown in from Berlin, paced the floor. Chernoff crumpled the paper he held in his hand and threw it at Clovich cringing behind the desk.

"You call this a report, Comrade?" he shouted as he leaned over the desk. Clovich dreaded that word, *Comrade.* He knew Chernoff only used that word in a derogatory sense or as a threat. "Our best agent in Europe doesn't return from a simple mission of surveillance and disruption of an American schoolboy and you don't have an explanation? Come, come, Comrade, you can do better than that."

"Our sources in London told us that Parker would be alone on assignment in Norway," Clovich tried to explain. "He was to visit Bergen, Alesund, and Trondheim. Antoine signaled that he had picked him up in Alesund and that was the last we heard. A small article in the Trondheim newspaper mentioned that an unidentified passenger was reported lost at sea from the fast boat near Kristiansund. We must assume that Antoine is dead."

"Are you telling me that Parker took Antoine out? My instructions were clear. This was not a wet assignment, just put a little scare into Parker."

"Something must have gone terribly wrong. There was no indication that Parker's mission was critical. My guess is that another agent met him. There must have been a confrontation and Antoine came out second best."

"That is a stupid theory, comrade. I'm holding you personally responsible for Antoine's loss. To be taken out by an amateur is totally absurd. I'll review your status here with my superiors in Berlin. In the meantime, recheck your sources in London and see if we can find out what really happened. If we can't rely on their information, tell them that I'll shake the whole organization until their teeth rattle."

Chernoff was rightfully disturbed. Antoine was one of his best agents and had a solid record of besting the German Gestapo throughout WWII. Parker was either extremely lucky or more highly trained than he had presumed. He vowed to make him pay dearly for Antoine's death, but knew he had to be patient. Waiting for the precise moment to do the most damage to the London CIA Office was important.

"I want a weekly report in detail on what's going on in London, particularly focusing on Parker," Chernoff barked for emphasis. "Put some heat on our sources. We can't let London get away with taking out one of our agents without retaliation. Get someone else ready to move on Parker when I give the word."

"Yes, comrade Chernoff," Clovich replied. He took a notebook out to make notes. He scribbled something just for show. What he needed now was another top agent.

* * *

The next few weeks were idyllic for Parker. The weekly mission to Copenhagen was a breeze. Maybe Smythe was right for once about a routine mission.

He wanted to move in with Airy, but the Embassy wouldn't permit it. They weren't too happy about his romance, but they put up with it. Once Airy had broken through whatever initially held her back, she became an accomplished lover. At first James was the tutor, but soon Airy, the pupil, was becoming the orchestrater. She slowly took charge.

"James, I love you," she would moan in all different tones and intonations. Parker would verbally respond in kind, but could never quite match her fervor. "James, I want to get married."

Reality set in immediately. Parker wasn't quite ready for this. Navy regulations provided a convenient roadblock. Men in the armed services still had to have their commanding officer's permission to marry a non-citizen overseas. James explained, "There is no way they would give permission while I am on assignment with the Embassy. Airy, the Korean truce seems to be holding and they won't hold the Reservists for more than six months. By Christmas everything should be settled, and I'll come back for you."

"All sailors say that, but they never do," Airy retorted. She definitely was not convinced. "James, get me the visa papers from the Embassy. I have a cousin in Pittsburgh who will sponsor me. We'll have time in the States to have a decent wedding."

Falling in love with Airy was easy for Parker. Making a marriage commitment was difficult. Besides, risks in what he was now doing for the embassy made making plans impossible.

For the weekly runs to Copenhagen, Parker was operating out of Conrad's apartment and took many devious routes to the airport. His confidence grew and he felt reasonably sure that no one was following him. Conrad was in the loop on this one so there was no need to be evasive.

"Do you ever read any of those books you carry back and forth?" Conrad asked.

"Sometimes I read a chapter or two en route to Copenhagen. There's never enough in the book to really grab my interest. They have a lot of biographies that I'm not really interested in. So far I haven't let my curiosity get the better on the way back. If I opened any of those books, I'd probably mess up a code or lose something important. They keep telling me it's better to know as little as possible about what I'm carrying, and so far it seems to be working out."

"Copenhagen is a good R and R stop. Are any of those big busted Danish darlings giving Airy competition?" Chad taunted.

"Not on your life. I use Thursdays to rest up so I can keep Airy happy for the next six days."

Chad shrugged his shoulders, "You're just no fun anymore, James. I have to take care of the clerical help at the Embassy all by myself."

"What's going on with Natasha?" Parker interjected. It wasn't her real name, but Parker liked to make up exotic names for Conrad's Russian Embassy target.

"I got a few things out of her," Chad answered.

"I'll bet you got more than a few things into her. I hope you keep your mouth shut about what goes on around here. That dame may be working you more than you're working her."

"Now how can I keep my mouth shut if my mission is to ply her with sex?"

"Ask Evans, he seems to have an answer for everything. By the way, see if you can get her out of the flat early enough on Friday so I can change clothes and get back to the Wellington without embarrassing both Embassies."

Chad thought for a moment for the last line. "I think I'll tell her next time to answer the door naked. She has a secret map of Russia tattooed right below her belly button that I haven't been able to decode yet. Maybe you can help."

Parker smiled. On second thought, maybe he could help Chad, but right now he needed to get moving if he was going to pick up his books and make the morning flight to Copenhagen.

Eric picked him up at the airport. "Did you have a nice flight, Mr. Parkinson?"

Parker did not appreciate Evans' humor in keeping his passport in the Parkinson name. "Easy for you to remember," Evans gave as an excuse.

"Lots of clouds and turbulence. This must be more like the summers in Europe I read about years ago. It amazes me how the Allied bombers ever found their targets in Germany."

Parker relaxed as he leaned back in his seat in the taxi. "Eric, take me straight to the Neptune Hotel today. I've got only one stop this afternoon. I'm taking a customer out to dinner tonight at the Tivoli so I won't need you in town. Pick me up at the hotel Friday for the airport at the usual time."

Eric raised his hand to his head as if to salute that he understood.

Parker had been given specific instructions for tonight.

"Take the proprietor of the Bookmark Store for dinner at the best restaurant at the Tivoli Gardens," Smythe had told him. "Stroll around the gardens later. Go to the High Striker, the mallet and bell ringer stall, and try your luck. The vendor will know who you are. Stay in the garden until after the fireworks, then depart."

Peter Blixen was a man of rotund proportions. He had been in the book business for twenty years. During the war, he set up a book exchange business in the heart of Copenhagen. English books were a prized commodity.

"Those books you bring me are awful, Josh. They don't sell. I don't know how you can afford to take me to dinner." Blixen said as he lifted a piece of steak with his fork."

"Look at it as a kind of investment, Peter," Parker replied. "Some day I'll bring you a book that will be a best seller and that will make both you and me rich." He sipped his Aquavit. He was going to miss these dinners when the assignment is over.

"How long have you been working the book shuttle out of London?"

"Not long. I did some photography for National Geographic but it didn't work out. This job opened up, so I decided to stay in London." The lies came easily, but it was time to change the subject before he got into trouble. "The fireworks are special tonight. Is there a holiday?"

"Yes, I think it might be St. Olaf's day."

Blixen told tales about the food shortages during the war and how they played tricks on the Germans. Parker was patient, sipping Cherry Herring. There was no struggle over the check. Parker took it and added an extra tip courtesy of the American Embassy.

Parker steered Blixen towards the south end of the Gardens. He had seen the High Striker stand before but never paid much attention to it. The object was to swing this huge mallet at a target that would propel a weight upward towards a large bell about twelve feet above the bottom stand. The vendor was making his pitch in Danish to a group of six Danes to try their luck, but they seemed more interested in their beer and watching for tight skirts. He spotted Parker.

"You, you, come over," he shouted in English. "You look like an American. Try your luck."

Parker approached handing the vendor a Danish bill and then grabbed the mallet. It must have weighed twenty-five pounds, enough to throw him off balance if he wasn't careful.

The Danes staggered forward to take a look at the performance. Compared to Parker they were all giants.

Parker took the mallet up carefully. He was more interested in hitting the spot than in swinging it with force. He was right on target. The weight flew up and made contact with the bell, startling many of the strollers along the path.

"See, this puny American can ring the bell," the man chanted as he grabbed the mallet from Parker.

"You sir, you, it's your turn to protect the honor of Denmark." He grabbed the largest Dane by the arm. The Dane came forward and a smirk crossed his mouth as he looked down on Parker. He took a firm stance swinging the mallet wide and the force of the impact seemed to shake the ground. The weight barely made it up two thirds of the way.

In true carnival fashion, the man worked the crowd taking in their money. Only one contestant made the bell ring. Parker and Blixen stayed to watch. They were fascinated how the vendor could play on the ego of men.

When the crowd ebbed, the man called to Parker. "You did very well," he said with a wide grin. "You were a winner. Pick a prize." He motioned him towards the stand.

"Some day you'll have to tell me how you fixed the game for me." Parker looked over the row of some twenty small dolls and picked one out.

"Peter, give this to one of your granddaughters. Tell them that you won it at the Tivoli."

The fireworks began. Peter was pleased with the evening. So was Parker.

* * *

The days were getting shorter. Chernoff's office on the west side of the Berlin complex was exceptionally cold this morning. Heat wasn't turned on until the middle of October. With his good leg, he kicked the radiator in disgust.

"Ivan!" he shouted. "Ivan get in here!"

The door burst open. "Yes, Comrade Chernoff. What can I do for you?"

"Get me some of my special coffee," he ordered. It was made from illegal beans he had personally smuggled back from West Berlin. Along with an ounce of Vodka, it would warm his bones.

"Yes, Comrade Chernoff."

He returned to reading the latest reports from Paris. Information was flowing steadily about American troop location and strength in Germany. Agents were tracking food and oil supplies, which had proven to be extremely reliable. No change in allocations was noted during the June uprising. Situation reports on July and August remained the same. He was glad to forward these calming reports to Moscow, but was troubled by one notation. One of the operatives said he sensed some change in attitudes of his contact and asked to have a security check made.

If there was trouble, it had to be Paris, Chernoff deduced. All the field reports were gathered in Paris and then sent to Berlin by diplomatic pouch. There might be a leak in the KGB Station in Paris that had not been operating smoothly since Antoine disappeared.

Chernoff picked up the London report. Parker made weekly trips to some Copenhagen bookstores and that was all. Their agent in Copenhagen wormed his way into a part time job at one of the shops, but couldn't detect any messages in the books given to Parker. The report also noted that Parker had received special instructions about this week's trip, but mentioned no further details. There had to be a connection with the uneasiness reported from Paris.

It was time to move on Parker. Chernoff pressed the buzzer. "Get me a ticket for Copenhagen for Thursday morning. Have Vladimir pick me up at the airport."

CHAPTER FOURTEEN

Chad Conrad was the last member of the staff to give a report during the Monday morning update in Jack Evan's office.

"Nice report, Chad, but no substance. Get some hard information or point your work in another direction." Evans paused and looked at Chad for effect. "That's it for today, gentlemen. Smythe, can you stick around for a few minutes?"

The room cleared. Smythe refilled his coffee cup and sought out a more conformable chair.

"Heidi has finally got the info on who has been tipping off the Russians on our troop movements in Germany," Evans began. "She's got him nailed along with a list of accomplices and signaled that she is ready to make a drop."

"It's about time. Parker's been in position for five weeks. I was afraid we'd run out of expense money the way he's spreading it around."

"She's on her way to Copenhagen now for her holiday. Another live drop between them would be too dangerous," Evans continued. "I don't want to take a chance that a dead drop might go wrong either."

Smythe smirked. He caught the gist of the message. "So that's why we set up the carni man…. to be the cut out. That's one of the oldest tricks in the books. If the Russians are tailing Parker, do you think they're stupid enough to fall for it?"

Evans countered, "I'm betting they think Parker's too stupid to get away with it even if we tried it."

"I wouldn't bet on that." Smythe finished his coffee. "He's waiting in my office now. I'll do my best to walk him through what he has to do."

"We need this drop to be a clean one, Smythe, so coach him through it thoroughly. I don't want those names compromised."

"You mean to tell me that for the past five weeks I've been carrying books back and forth to Copenhagen and there hasn't been a damn thing in them?" Parker sputtered.

"That's right. It's all a set up to throw the Russians off track. If they have you under surveillance, we figure they'll be getting bored by now," Smythe answered.

"I've been looking for ghosts around every corner and you and your CIA buddies have just been playing a game. I've had a death grip on those damn books and there's nothing in them!" Parker slumped in his seat. "I can't believe you did that."

"Everything we do has a plan, Parker," Smythe said slowly for effect. "We don't tell you everything. You knew that from the very beginning."

` Parker shook his head. "This is crazy."

"Not so. The real drop will be made Friday morning. It should be routine."

"Routine!" Parker exploded from his chair. "I'm getting sick and tired of that word. Nothing has been routine since I've gotten here. Even the book routine was a hoax."

"All right, Lieutenant." Smythe retrieved his command voice for a moment. "You're still in the Navy. Now, sit down and listen." This was the first time he had seen Parker show a burst of outward emotion. He was seething but still was in control. Smythe liked what he saw.

"This drop is too sensitive for you to meet with the agent. Since you may be under surveillance, a dead drop it's too risky so we're going to use a cut out."

Parker shook his head indicating that he did not understand.

"An intermediary. The cut out is the carni man at the High Striker booth. He'll be the buffer between you and the agent. Just after lunch Friday, go to his stand. He'll rig the chute so you win. He'll hand you a stuffed doll. Inside will be a small plastic container the size of your thumb. That's what we want. Bring it back."

"What about those dumb books?"

"Go through the motions, just like before. If we have any luck, the books will throw them off."

"I still can't believe you made me go through all that stuff with the books for all those weeks for nothing."

"Parker, we hope it wasn't for nothing."

"You don't look very happy today, Lieutenant," Penelope observed. "Things all right in Copenhagen?"

"Yeah, just dandy," Parker answered with cynicism. He sat on the corner of her desk trying to calm down. He picked up the porcelain ballerina he bought her on his first trip to Copenhagen and turned it around in his hand. "Another week, another trip. Make the same reservations. I'll stop in Wednesday to pick them up."

"Aye aye, sir," Penelope responded trying to take the edge off.

Parker put the figurine down and gave a half salute good bye. He was on his way to Airy's flat.

On Mondays Airy worked late. It was a restocking day. Most of the new merchandise came in over the weekend, so Airy had to check the packing slips with the orders and direct the goods to the correct departments. Selfridges was beginning to rely more and more on Airy's talents in buying women's wear.

Parker took some delight in cooking dinner on Mondays. His experience of fending for himself as a youngster made him an adequate, if not gourmet, cook. He was into stir frying some lamb bits. He whistled "Elmer's Tune" to lighten up his spirits in the dismally furnished flat as Airy burst through the door.

She had her shoes in her hand and flung them into a corner while gliding toward the couch in almost a single motion. "What a day!" she sighed as she looked up at Parker. He bent over and gave her an avuncular kiss. "How was your day, Jimmy?"

"Goofed off all day," he answered as he flopped down alongside her.

"You're mean!"

Dinner was quiet and it was obvious that Airy had more on her mind than the usual travails of a Monday.

"Mr. Harrington called me into his office today," Airy began the after dinner conversation.

"Who's Harrington?" asked James

"He's one of the vice-presidents of Selfridges?"

"Did he ask you for a date?"

"James, I'm serious."

171

Parker put his cup down to take on the appearance of being interested.

"He said he was impressed by my work and was considering me for a chief buyer position. This would encompass the entire line of women's clothing. He asked if I was interested."

"And what did you tell him?"

"I told him I'd have to think about it. It's a lot of responsibility. Longer hours, more traveling."

"Tell him you're interested. You've got the talent and brains."

"That's not it, James!" A furrow appeared on her unwrinkled forehead. Her tone changed to a demand. "I want to get married and go to America with you, James."

"Airy, I thought we had this settled. I should be out of the Navy shortly. I'll get a job, send for you, and we'll get married. Go after that new position, even if it's only for a few months. It'll be good experience and keep you busy while I get settled."

"It's not that simple, James. Selfridges is like a family. These moves are long-term commitments. You don't take a new assignment if you don't expect to be around six months from now. It's disloyal. You may do that in America, but it's just not done here."

"Then you'll have to hang in there for another six months."

Airy pursed her lips, then took another sip of tea. "Mother called yesterday. She questioned me on the wedding plans. She thinks you are stalling."

"That's not true. You know the Navy has strict rules on overseas marriages."

"I know of several girls who have married Americans without any problems."

"They weren't working for the Embassy, I'll bet."

"I don't even know what you are doing there. Other than a lot of traveling, what makes you different?"

"You know everything I do is classified and I'm not allowed to discuss it. Military personnel need permission to marry from their commanding officer. My CO isn't even at the Embassy."

"Chad is the only person I've met from the Embassy. I'm totally in the dark. Maybe Mum is right. You are stalling."

"Chad is working on your visa right now. Everyone knows I am seeing you. Look, there's a small reception at the Embassy next week for a new British Liaison Officer. I'll see about permission to bring you. You'll get a chance to meet Commander Smythe. He's as close to being my CO as you can get." He reached across the table and took her hand. "I love you, Airy. Please be patient."

Airy squeezed his hand but slowly shook her head.

Eric had transported Parker to three bookstores in Copenhagen this Friday morning. Parker made deliveries to the first two and they had no returns. The third customer ordered several books but had a single book to return. It sat on the table next to his lunch at his favorite restaurant in the Tivoli Gardens

The weather was cool and overcast. He needed the fresh air to keep his thinking clear. It was well past noon, and he felt uneasy about this drop. If it was "routine", then why the five weeks of work setting him up as a book salesman. His appetite was not there this afternoon and he pushed the sandwich away. He'd much prefer to have lunch with Airy at the Selfridges Cafeteria.

"Is the smorgasbord not good today, sir?" the waiter asked.

"No, everything's just fine." Parker motioned for the check. As he was about to get up, he took a look around. No suspicious characters. The music from the bandstand played a familiar melody, yet he still felt something was wrong. Maybe he was losing his touch.

There was only a small crowd around the High Striker. Two young couples with children stood close by. One of the fathers was taking a swing when the carni man spotted Parker. As the young father was receiving condolences for not ringing the bell, Parker edged closer and handed the vendor some money. He placed his briefcase down and set his book on top of it then moved forward and grabbed the mallet.

"Keep your eye on this man," the vendor announced in English.

Three figures in the background were doing just that. Chernoff was whispering to one of them. His sources in London had told him something important was to happen today but had given no other details. He didn't want to miss the opportunity of being present as they brought Parker down.

As Parker began to swing the mallet, the carni moved away and stealthily tapped a lever on the side of the machine with his foot. The weight shot upward like a rocket and rang the bell.

The children applauded.

"You are a winner!" As the carni handed Parker a small stuffed doll, one of the men in the background moved smoothly into the crowd and snatched the book off the brief case so deftly that no one noticed. The thief moved away out of sight.

Chernoff remained in place with the second man and continued to watch Parker for a mistake.

After accepting the accolades of the crowd, Parker picked up his briefcase and stuffed the doll in his pocket. It appeared that he had forgotten all about the book.

The picture registered on Chernoff. He grabbed the second man pulling him close. "It's not the book; it's the doll!" All pretense of subtlety was dropped. The two men menacingly closed in. The carni man gave a directional twist of his head. Parker turned and recognized the Russian from their previous meeting in Copenhagen, but didn't back away. As they came closer Parker withdrew the doll from his pocket, bent over to a young girl of about three, and handed it to her. Her eyes widened with joy as her father, unsuccessful in his attempt to earn a doll, said, "Thank you." with a deep Danish accent.

Parker then spun putting the family between the two aggressors and him and started to walk away. The second man reached down and snatched the doll from the girl, only to be stunned with an elbow to the head from her father knocking the doll out of his hand. Moving in quickly, Chernoff drew his revolver but kept it close to his chest so it was visible only to the father. "Be careful. Your little girl more precious than the doll." The Dane grabbed his daughter and promptly retreated with his family.

Chernoff picked up the doll and squeezed it. There was no container. He examined the doll. One side was torn open. "That son-of-a-bitch has it on him!" He shoved his companion in the direction Parker had moved, but it was too late. He was nowhere to be seen

"Don't worry, Vladimir, he won't get away," Chernoff assured. "We have a back-up plan."

Eric was in his cab waiting by the North entrance. "Let's go," Parker shouted as he jumped into the cab.

"To the airport?"

"Not today. To the train station. I think the weather is closing in. I'm going to take the train to Amsterdam and maybe take the ferry back to London in a day or two."

The early morning Saturday edition of the *London Times* was slipped under Parker's door of his room at the Admiral Krasnapolsky. On the second page, there was a short note. "BOAC flight 343 from Copenhagen to London was canceled due to mechanical problems discovered shortly after it had lined up on the tarmac for takeoff. All passengers disembarked and were assigned other flights."

Well, not all passengers.

The debriefing session on the Copenhagen drop took place Saturday in Evans' office. Both Foxworthy and Smythe were present.

"What possessed you to extract the vial from the doll so quickly?" Evans asked.

"I really don't know. Maybe instinct. I felt uneasy about this assignment from the moment Commander Smythe briefed me on it. They were waiting for me at the airport, weren't they?" Parker looked at the three faces, seeking out a reaction. There was none. "There was no way they were going to let me on that plane with that vial. Am I right?"

"Now we don't know that for sure," Evans replied, attempting to fend off the questions.

"There's got to be a leak somewhere. They were at the High Striker in Tivoli before I was. Somebody set me up." Parker looked around. "They would have killed me if they had to."

Smythe spoke in defense. "Jack has been running you himself to ensure your safety. There were less people than normal involved with this kind of drop."

"With all due respect, sir, that's bullshit. Under no circumstances could the Russians be there by coincidence. They went after that doll like the proverbial hound dog after a bitch in heat. They knew the time and place and all they had to do was watch the carni guy to pick out the right doll."

"We'll check everything again, just be careful what you say and to whom. We'll see if we can schedule some very ordinary runs to some of the Embassies on the continent to see if things cool down.

Parker took a deep breath. Shit, he knew what was coming next.

"You're dismissed, Lieutenant.

CHAPTER FIFTEEN

Smythe casually leafed through a file spread out in front of him. He had never really taken the time to study Parker's Top Secret Clearance. The folder contained a series of routine FBI interviews with relatives and associates. All seemed to be extremely positive. He paused, then suddenly became more interested.

Maternal grandparents were traced to Kolochko, a small village near Kocise in Southwestern Czechoslovakia. They were dirt poor farmers. Kocise grabbed his attention. It was just 33 kilometers from the Russian Ukraine. Paternal grandparent's roots were traced to Hernard-Petri in Hungary, Just 42 kilometers from Kocise. They also were farmers.

Smythe closed the folder and headed to Evans' office.

"I think we've stumbled across the solution to our problem in the Kiev sector," Smythe said as he passed the folder to Evans. "Would you believe, Parker's ancestry goes back to the corner of Slovakia wedged between Poland, Russia, and Hungary. His profile makes him physically fit into the area like a native. He'd be a cinch to make the live drop of the Minox."

Evans did a speed read of the folder, then looked up at Smythe. "The timing couldn't be better."

* * *

The People's University in Kiev was an unlikely site for international intrigue. At best, its buildings were shabby and still showed damage suffered during the war. Located in the heart of Russia's breadbasket, the college specialized in agricultural research focusing on organic chemistry. Fertilizers topped the research list. All this changed when deposits of Uranium were discovered in nearby Hungary.

Dr. Yuri Karin, the head of the Chemistry department, had survived the war. His position at the university along with an extensive knowledge of nitrates made him an unexpected expert in explosives. That plus his age kept him out of the front lines during the war. However, to his credit, he did pick up a rifle from a fallen Russian soldier to help rout the retreating Germans from the University grounds in 1943.

Karin headed up a team of scientists assigned the task of determining the quickest and most efficient means of extracting enough U238 isotopes from its parent U235. To make a critical mass for Russia's first version of an atomic bomb, crude costly methods were used and not enough U238 was being produced to create an arsenal. Several of his colleagues on campus were involved in the project as well as two German scientists who were indentured in Kiev. The pair seemed to be contributing; as well they should, since retribution on their families in Eastern Germany was always a threat.

The Rosenbergs had done their work well with specific information on the detonation mechanics of the bomb with details coming directly from Los Alamos. Missing were the particulars on the extraction process for uranium isotope being developed in Oak Ridge, Tennessee. Some data was available, but what the Americans were actually using was still a mystery. Whatever it was, it was effective since considerable quantities of U238 converted into Plutonium were flowing into Los Alamos.

Karin stood at the blackboard surrounded by his team of Russians and imported Germans. He was outlining his favorite path, the centrifuge method to take advantage of the difference in weights between the two isotopes. The more conventional method of precipitation-filtration process was so far unsuccessful. The Germans favored a new ion exchange method that was not mentioned at all by the Rosenbergs.

"Moscow wants our theoretical work completed in the next two weeks and a schematic of the process next month," Yuri stated as he rapped the chalk against the board. "I would suggest we adjourn for the day and concentrate on arriving at a conclusion by Monday. We don't want to disappoint Moscow."

The group was not pleased, but the thought of a winter in Siberia compared to the mildly temperate winters of Kiev was a great incentive to meet the deadline.

The Soviet system suited Karin well. It provided him with a chair at the University, which included a modest, but stable income with a few perks. It wasn't disillusionment with the system that turned him into an informant for the West. It was money.

Sex was Yuri Karin's only vice. He didn't smoke, drink, or gamble but the urge for sexual conquest was beyond his control. Besides a submissive wife, he subsidized a mistress. It was costing him more than his University salary could provide, so he contacted an attaché in the Swiss Consulate who was already heavily in the business of setting up bank accounts for corrupt Soviet officials. In exchange for a few notes on the status of the Russian uranium project forwarded to the CIA, a small but steady flow of cash had been provided. The Americans were beginning to press for more detail, but the Swiss contact was reluctant to transport more than a single sheet and then only at irregular intervals via dead drops. A way was needed to condense the documents.

It was the beginning of the fall semester. As Department Head, Karin was only required to teach one chemistry class and a lab. The sophomore class he chose was large and was a proving ground to weed out the borderline students.

Among the students was 19 year old Anna Dropnov for whom her college scholarship provided a corridor away from the wretchedly poor farm life she had grown to hate. As a young girl she and her parents welcomed the Germans in 1942 on the promise of a better life. All too soon it was obvious that the farmers were trading a bad system for virtual slavery. After the war, the farmers' situation grew worse. The more you produced, the more the state took away. Farming held no future for Anna. Her striking good looks coupled with better than average intelligence won her the right to a paid freshman year at the University. The real test was her sophomore year where she needed to be in the top ten percent of the class to continue her stipend. A good grade in Chemistry was crucial.

Anna took a seat in the first row of stations in the laboratory. The first lecture was perfunctory. Lab assignment books were distributed and Dr. Karin went over the laboratory safety rules.

"Are there any questions?" he asked. No hands went up.

"Class is dismissed."

Anna took her time in gathering up her things and when most of the students were gone, she took a step forward.

"Could I talk to you for a moment?" she asked.

Not looking up, Yuri answered as if it were a well-versed chant, "Make an appointment for time during my office hours."

Anna sighed, and turned to leave as Yuri looked up. He recognized the young woman as being seated just a few steps away from the lectern. Dark black hair, fine features, and her shapely leg had caught his eye. Her skirt was remarkably tight, accenting her hips as she moved away.

"Just a minute. You can walk back to my office with me."

Anna joined stride with him. "I am very worried about Chemistry, Dr. Karin. I had all superior grades as a freshman, but my high school had no courses in Chemistry. I may be behind the other students and I need a good grade to maintain my scholarship."

"If you apply yourself, you should have no trouble," Karin replied in a less than convincing tone.

"Professor Karin, is there any way I could earn extra credit?"

Yuri opened his office door and motioned Anna in. He already knew the answer. He placed his books on the desk and sat down.

"Close the door, Anna."

His gaze told her what he had in mind. She closed the door and came up close to the desk, paused for a moment, then started to unfasten the top of her blouse.

"No time for that," he instructed as he motioned her to come behind his desk. He slowly took her head in his hands and brought her to a kneeling position. He unzipped his pants and took out his already engorged penis. Anna was initially taken aback by his brashness, then nodded acceptance. As she took the penis into her mouth, he began to concentrate on a complex chemical formula trying to postpone ejaculation, but it did no good. She was too beautiful and evidently had some previous practice.

After laboratory classes Anna stayed to help straighten up. Yuri's office was out of the question for any more liaisons since no locks were permitted on any office doors. The lab was another matter since it had a lock as a safety precaution. Anna knew the ritual. She would simply be sure to wear no underwear on lab days. It was a simple matter to bend over the lab table. Her groans were coordinated with his thrusts so she was either enjoying the sex or she was the consummate actress. Regardless which it was, Yuri didn't care.

"Dr. Karin, we can't continue doing this. If we are found out, I'll lose my scholarship and you will be demoted. You must get us a room somewhere where we can meet with no chance of discovery," Anna said as she kissed him on the cheek.

Yuri looked at Anna. She was too perfect to give up. He had become addicted to her as if she had been cocaine. .

"I'll think of something."

He needed more money.

Karin left the signal that the next drop had been made. The Swiss made the retrival unnoticed on his way to his office. This time there were no formulas or schematics, just a note.

Get me a camera and double the money.

CHAPTER SIXTEEN

"This is our latest weapon," Albert Whitehall said as he held up the Minox camera. Measuring only about ¾ inches square by three inches long, it was small enough to be easily concealed. "This is one of the rare original Riga models. The lens has a fixed aperture as is the exposure speed. This leaves the focal length also fixed with a very narrow focal width. That means that this camera is a single use device. To properly photograph an 8 ½ by 11-inch standard paper size, the distance must be exactly 13 inches. Let me show how this works."

Whitehall laid out a memo sheet and positioned a lamp nearby. He slid the camera open extending its length to about 5 inches. Holding the camera with his right hand above the document while his elbow was on the table, he unreeled a wire from the camera. He then tilted his right arm until the wire settled on the paper.

"The wire is that critical 13 inches in length, and the elbow on the table will keep the camera steady." Whitehall pressed the shutter release then closed the camera. "This action advances the film and prevents any double exposures. Each shot is about ¼ inch square and a roll of film provides 50 exposures."

"Riga. Isn't that somewhere in Latvia?" Parker asked.

"Yes. It started out as a rich man's toy, but now the Germans are making them."

Whitehall handed the camera to Parker. "Here. You try a couple of shots. We'll see how good you are when they're developed."

Parker took several shots, trying to use the viewfinder while carefully positioning the camera to 13 inches. He then handed the camera back to Whitehall.

"Looks like a snap."

"Your assignment is to deliver the Minox camera to an agent in a town called Kocise in the eastern corner of Czechoslovakia," Evans told Parker. "There's a minimum risk since you should blend into the community with no trouble. We're betting that no one will question your presence since you are a look-alike with both your grandparents coming from that location. Remember, blend in. That's your job. You will go from Vienna to Kocise with an Austrian passport listing you as a student with a visa to attend a Chemical Engineering Conference being held there. By now your German should get you past the borders. Keep a low profile in Czechoslovakia."

Parker nodded.

"Your contact is a man about 50. He has your description. The code is 'The sky', then a three second pause, 'is blue.' Your response is 'The sea', another three second pause, then 'is also blue.' The pauses are absolutely essential."

"The sky, one thousand, two thousand, three thousand, is blue," Parker mocked.

Evans did not find that amusing, but continued outlining the mission.

"What makes this live drop necessary is that you must spend time with the contact demonstrating how to operate the camera, otherwise the drop is worthless. And for God's sakes, Parker, blend in. Blend in."

Higgins had requisitioned some Eastern European clothes and a student's backpack from some unknown cache.

"These should be the right size," Higgins said. "I picked these out special for you. Try them on."

Parker was not sure what Higgins meant by that remark, but he ignored it and slipped into the shoes. They were more comfortable than he expected.

"These shoes have a few miles on them." he commented.

"You're supposed to be student, not a professor. Here's your camera."

He handed Parker a black bullet shaped plastic tube that had a string necklace emerging from its top.

"Wear this around your neck as an amulet. Students do crazy things like this."

Parker examined the container and tried to unscrew what he thought was a cap on the square end. It wouldn't budge.

"Is this thing glued shut?"

"No, but we put a left hand thread on it. Maybe others will try to open it the way you did if they suspect anything.

"This is an odd shape."

"It's made like that so it can be easily concealed."

"I don't understand."

Higgins gave a closed mouth grin while Parker did some thinking.

"No way!" Parker said in disbelief.

"It's called cavity concealment. It's been done before."

"Not by this sailor."

CHAPTER SEVENTEEN

The Ambassador's limo left the Embassy at 10 a.m. There was a scheduled briefing with the Prime Minister at 10:30. The meetings were used to bring the U.S. up to date on diplomatic issues. The Ambassador already knew what to expect since he had a source very high up in the British chain of command, but he had to pretend to be surprised. Besides, the lunches were always good.

The limo sped away from number 10 Downing Street, making several quick turns. Assuring himself that he wasn't being followed, the driver turned around to the back seat.

"The next stop light, duck out, sir."

Parker had been flat on the floor. Evans wanted to be sure that he got out of the Embassy without being observed. The limo drew to a stop.

"This is it. Good luck."

Parker opened the door and literally rolled out the limo door staying stooped over till he got to the front of the car. He then stood straight and proceeded to the sidewalk as if he were simply crossing the street.

Dressed in well-worn casual clothes and a khaki backpack, he felt uncomfortable and out of place. When Higgins had provided the clothes, Parker put them on to check the fit. Higgins couldn't help commenting on his handiwork. "You look like a nineteen year old college kid. Now, if we could just add a few pimples." The uneasiness left him once he saw that no one was paying the least bit of attention to him.

Parker took a tourist class seat on a Lufthansa flight from London to Munich. The weather was overcast as he crossed the channel. It seemed to herald the coming fall season. From there he traveled by train to Vienna second class spending most of his time practicing his German on his fellow passengers in the compartment.

Using an Austrian passport, Parker tried to feign sleepiness when custom officials boarded the train at the borders on the way to Vienna so he could answer their questions with a simple *Ja* or *Nein*. Other papers included registration at the University of Vienna, a student identification card, and information on the Annual Chemical Society Convention in Czechoslovakia. He had three days left before the contact appointment so he stayed over a night each in Vienna and Budapest in two star hotels before he headed for Kocise. He bought a Czech phrase book in Vienna to study while on the train. Seemingly not attracting any attention, he started to relax, and only occasionally handled the black amulet that hung around his neck. He was sure not to shave or wash up. He wanted not only to look like a student, but also to smell like one.

Yuri Karin always looked forward to the Chemical Society Convention in Kocise. He wasn't presenting any papers, but he enjoyed communicating with his professional peers outside of Russia. Most of the participants were from the Eastern Block, but some attendees were also chemists from Austria,

Switzerland, and France. Besides, he had a long time female acquaintance to round out his evenings with, so when his Swiss contact instructed him on the live drop in Kocise, he was eager to comply.

The train trip from Kiev to Uhzorod, the Russian border town, was unbelievably slow. While Italy could brag that Mussolini got the trains to run on time, the Soviets could not boast of such an accomplishment. The 300-mile trip took over 10 hours giving Karin time to look over his traveling companions. He was virtually alone in the first class compartment, and no one took the initiative to strike up a conversation.

There was no need for the conductor to announce the upcoming town of Uhzorod. The lack of proper sewage disposal gave the town a unique smell that could be recognized an hour away. A bus was waiting at the station to take passengers into Czechoslovakia for the 60-mile ride to Kocise. Karin noticed a single passenger get off a second class car and head for the bus. The man, wearing a light brown overcoat, was overdressed for lower class ticket. In Kocise he departed from the bus along with Karin, but then disappeared down the street.

The convention was to be held at the Hotel Slovan in the center of Kocise. Visiting students stayed in a dormitory hotel two blocks away called the Akademia. There Parker waited in line to present his pre-registered papers at the desk, received his convention tickets, and then made his way upstairs. The rooms were for four students. He wandered around until he found an empty bunk, put his backpack there, then followed some students to the cafeteria. Most of the students were speaking Russian, Hungarian, or Slavic dialects. Once they found out he spoke only German, they paid no attention to him.

Most of the papers presented the next day at the Hotel Slovan were not in German, but Parker took a notebook from his backpack and scribbled any mathematical formulae as if he was an interested student. He was concentrating on the 7 p.m. mass at the St. Elizabeth Cathedral about a kilometer away where he was to meet his contact.

As the church bells rang announcing evening services, Parker was walking down St. Elizabeth's main aisle looking for special pews on the left where Evans told him to sit. Originally these pews were constructed for the noblemen and contained a special leaning rail, also providing a good place to rest a bible. They were easy to spot, but the first row was occupied by several older women wearing babushkas. The second row had three women and a nondescript man. Parker sat next to the man. This must be the contact, since Evans had assured him it wasn't a woman like in Munich. He waited. The man ignored him.

Parker wanted to turn around to see if his contact might be somewhere else, but he did not dare do anything to attract attention. He spotted several other students from the dormitory. He glanced at the hands of the man to his left. He was holding a missal and his lips were moving in response to the priest's incantations. The priest faced the congregation and chanted something indistinguishable. As the congregation rose the man uttered, "The sky." Parker counted to himself one, one thousand, two, two thousand, three, three thousand. "Is blue," the man finished.

It was a game to cover the code by using the noise of the congregation changing its position. Parker waited until the priest made some sort of motion ordering everyone to sit. On the way down, Parker whispered, "The sea." He counted off the seconds, then said, "is also blue."

There was no recognition by the man to his left. Evans, as usual, had not given him any back up strategy so he had no choice but to wait. It was all up to the contact now.

Communion was being offered. The older people emptied the pews to receive the host. The younger people just sat back. When it came for his pew to go to the altar, the contact grabbed Parker's arm preventing him from standing, placed his missal in Parker's lap, rose, and proceeded toward the altar. The man received communion and vanished.

A message must be in the missal Parker thought as he flipped through the pages as fast as he could without attracting attention. There was no note. The organist began the recessional of the priest and the congregation began to sing. The sign directly below the pulpit had the list of songs for the mass. The last number was 461. It was like lightning had struck. He opened the missal to song 461. Penciled in was:

2200, Zlatz Ducat, Marta

Zlatz Ducat, the golden coin, was a small restaurant a short distance down an alley off the main street, Hlavna. It was only a few minutes past eight and too early for the rendezvous, so Parker strolled to the fountain in the epicenter of the city and sat on a stone bench. The sprays from the fountain jets were synchronized with music. As Parker looked at the younger adults around the display, he could see what Evans was driving at. The hair color, complexion, stature, and facial features all had similarities to his. He was blending in as instructed whether he planned to or not.

Several restaurants had sidewalk cafes and Parker slid into a vacant spot. "Pivo," he said to a waiter standing near by. Beer in any language was a useful word. The waiter asked him a question he didn't understand. Taking a guess, he said, "Pilsner" and made a sign with his hands for a big drink. The waiter acknowledged and turned towards the bar.

Martin Dziak was an engineering student from the Czech Technical University of Prague. He and two other fellow students were on their first field trip away from the University, so the convention was an adventure for them. They had just seated themselves in a prime location to ogle the attractive young women in extremely short skirts who strolled the main street of Kocise. Dziak recognized Parker from one of the lectures and rose to ask him to join them.

"*Nevim chesky*," Parker said trying to tell them that he didn't speak Czech. "*Ich bin deutsch*," he added.

Dziak shook his head. German was not a popular language once the WWII occupation ended. "Do you speak English?" he asked in halting words.

Parker thought for a split second. Maybe he could fake some English. He felt the need to not feel alone. "Yes—I speak a little."

"Good. Have some beer with us," Martin replied. He grabbed Parker's arm and pulled him up not allowing him to refuse the invitation.

The three students quickly were caught up in a game of whistles and taunts to tempt the passing young ladies to join them. Most of them didn't even turn to glance as they passed by. It seemed that the young, impoverished students drinking beer were not on their list for tonight.

The conversation in halting English with Czech translation for the other two students gave Parker time to carefully choose his English words in the present tense only. A pair of passing young girls had exceptionally tight skirts through which the lines of their panties showed. This set the trio into a frenzy.

"What you think of dat?" Dziak said to Parker as he drew the pattern of the under pants in the air with a finger.

"She is very—nice," Parker responded.

When Martin made the translation to his friends, they broke out in hysterical laughter. Something must have been lost in the translation, Parker thought. He was now focusing on his watch. It was time to go.

At half past nine, it was late for dinner at the Zlatz Ducat and only a few patrons remained to be served by a single waitress. To order, Parker just pointed to something on the menu.

"*Dobre?*" Parker asked using one of the few Slovak words he learned from his mother.

"*Ano,*" the waitress nodded indicating that it was indeed good and he hoped for the best. The veal and noodles were delicious. When the waitress presented the bill, Parker wrote out the message from the man in church on it. He then covered it with a 500-koruna note. When she returned with the change, Parker waved her to keep it. She smiled, nodded recognition, and she refilled his coffee cup tapping her finger on the table. Parker figured the next move was up to her.

After the last customer left, the woman motioned Parker to follow her. She led the way out a back entrance and up to the next floor. She was not young, but amply proportioned and obviously not just a waitress. A door opened into a small one room dimly lit flat. A bed, a couch, a small table, a two-burner stove, and a refrigerator about the size of a two-foot cube were the only furniture. A single bare light bulb burned overhead.

Without a word, the woman began to undress. Parker tried to tell her in scraps of German, English, and Slovak that he had business other than her, but she paid no attention. She continued to disrobe until she was nude, then climbed into bed, sat with her knees up, and pulled the covers up to her breasts. She just sat there and stared at him.

Parker was dumbfounded. Maybe he had gotten the message all wrong. Maybe this wasn't Marta. He never asked for her name. "Marta?" he asked almost frantically as he started towards her. Before she could answer, the door burst opened. Parker spun around to a half-crouched position, ready for anything, when a man in a short gray coat became visible. It was the contact from the Cathedral.

"Welcome to Eastern Europe," Yuri said softly in heavily accented English as he extended his hand. "We must work quickly as I am being followed."

"You scared the shit out of me," Parker blurted out. He let out a deep breath he had been holding. It didn't seem that the man understood his words, so he got right to the subject.

"Here it is," Parker said as he removed the vial from around his neck. The man made him edgy as he noticed beads of perspiration forming on the man's forehead. Parker hurriedly tried to unscrew the top of the vial, but it seemed to be stuck. Panic had momentarily blocked out that it was a left-hand thread; then he remembered and unscrewed the top

Parker briskly went through the routine that he had rehearsed with Whitehall. He then coached Yuri through each crucial step. "The light in this room is not enough. Get the paper near a lamp. Remember, keep it steady, at exactly the height of the chain, and get good light," Parker warned as he replaced the camera into the vial and handed it to Karin.

Yuri nodded then pulled Parker closer to him. "Remember, I want double the money."

Parker could see the desperation in the man's eyes. He could only guess what could drive a man to take such risks.

A loud knock on the door terminated his reflections. There was a rapid exchange of words through the door. Yuri tossed the vial to Marta, then pushed Parker toward the window.

"It's the police doing a security check."

CHAPTER EIGHTEEN

"Go out the window," Yuri whispered.

As the Russian went to open the door and Parker scurried to the open window and pulled himself over the sill and dropped to the roof just as he heard the click of the passkey. The roof was not what he expected. It was metal and there was nothing to hold onto. Parker was slowly, but quietly sliding down the roof. He tried to spread eagle to stop his slide, but gravity prevailed and there were no gutters to stop him. His silent fall into the darkened alleyway was broken by what seemed to be a passing pedestrian. The man, struck from above and behind, was reeling from the shock. He was in a policeman's uniform and he started to reach for his gun as he turned around.

Parker gave the surprised policeman an inspired sharp right punch to the solar plexus knocking the wind out him. He had no breath to cry out as Parker pulled his head down and delivered a knee to the chin dropping him to the ground with hardly a sound. He had given himself at least a sixty-second head start.

The distance from where he landed to the main street was 70 yards. In the 10 seconds it took in an all out sprint, Parker's mind raced equally as fast. His initial plan of reaching the train station and following the tracks south was dismissed in the first three seconds. The police would spot anyone running down Hlavna. Next plan? One second. The policeman he could not possibly identify him or figure out where he had come from. It was too dark, and everything happened so quickly. That took another two seconds. Evans instruction ignited in his brain: "Blend in!" Seven seconds gone. He pulled up with only a few yards to go and judiciously spent the remaining three seconds smoothing his hair and taking some leisurely strides onto Hlavna and past the line of sight from the restaurant.

He was in luck. His three student drinking partners were still at their table just a few yards away. As the seconds Parker was counting approached 60, he had grabbed a waiter and pulled him toward the table.

"*Pivo, pivo, pivo, pivo,*" Parker declared as he pointed out the three students and then himself. Greeted by cheers he slapped a 500-krouna note in the waiter's hand and took a seat. In the background, he heard some noise coming from the alley.

A moment later, a man in a tan coat followed by two policemen ran out and looked around. They stopped several people walking and asked questions rapidly. Their eyes darted among the pedestrians and into the several sidewalk cafes.

Parker had reached over and picked up one of the half filled glasses of beer and took a drink allowing some of the brew to trickle down his chin. Dziak gave him a surprised look dulled by too much beer, but then picked up his own glass. Parker touched his glass to Dziak's and said, "*Na zdravi!*" and everyone laughed.

He had a brief moment to look at his companions. Although he was at least five years older, the four of them could have passed for brothers. Maybe all of them were brothers in a sense.

The three men in pursuit gave his table only a moment's glance as they rapidly walked up town.

Parker relaxed. The waiter brought four new bottles and he poured the beer into his glass. He felt like he was home at last.

Martin Dziak became a friend for the next day's conference. Parker would ask him some questions in English and would pretend to jot them down in German. He left for Vienna at the close of the convention where he shopped for new clothes and checked into a first class hotel room with a private bath. He was getting to feel a desperate sense of isolation on these missions. The loneliness was getting to him. He needed to see Airy.

The return trip to London was uneventful.

* * *

The report on Parker was disturbing. He had disappeared. The London agent logged Parker into the Embassy, but never saw him exit. For some reason, the internal source was not responding. Something was going on. Chernoff had Ivan scour through incident reports throughout the continent to see if there was any hint of a mission Parker would have been assigned. Nothing was even in the slightest sense appeared suspicious.

Chernoff was infuriated that his London group had lost track of Parker. Since there was little chance of turning this courier, Parker would be taken out during his next assignment. It was time to put a punitive crimp in communications from the CIA Station in London.

All they had to do was find him.

CHAPTER NINETEEN

The debriefing session with Foxworthy, Smythe and Evans went smoothly. The camera had been delivered. Parker saw no need to mention the part where he slid off the roof.

There was a pause. "Your replacement should be here in ten days and you will be returning to your ship," Evans said coolly.

Parker looked at Foxworthy who acknowledged Evans' statement.

"You will make it back to the *Perry* just in time for its return to the States. With the Korean War armistice and the political situation stabilizing in the Far East, you should be released by Christmas."

Parker's jaw dropped. In his mind, he had been building a wall to block out the inevitable return to his ship. Although staying on at the Embassy with the hints of betrayal by a mole worried him, he had learned to like what he was doing. He never screwed up a mission and was getting better all the time. He had an unlimited expense account, stayed at the best hotels, had a love affair with a dream woman, and he had never felt more important in his life. A simple courier assignment had expanded into espionage and he was caught up in the drama. It was to end as quickly as it had begun. Parker slid back in his seat and stared at the wall.

"You've done a fine job for us and we appreciate it," Evans lauded. "Take the next few days off to wind down. We've notified Wellington Arms that you will be leaving. You may want to move your things out of Conrad's apartment. He knows your status. Penelope will make your travel arrangements back to the Med."

Parker snapped out of his trance. "Captain, request permission to move in with Airy for the rest of my time here. There shouldn't be a problem with security now that I'm headed back."

"I don't see any problem," Foxworthy replied. "Do you Evans?"

"No, perfectly OK. I understand you two are pretty serious."

"You might say that," Parker said trying to downplay his involvement. "You'll get a chance to meet her at the reception this evening."

"We'll be looking forward to it."

Smythe sat up in his chair. "That will be all, Lieutenant," he said signaling the end of the meeting. "Call my office daily next week just so we can keep track of you."

Parker left the office without his usual enthusiasm.

"I think we've got him," Evans said and both Smythe and Foxworthy nodded their agreement. "Wait until Wednesday, then spring it on him. I leave it in your hands, Smythe."

The plan had been hastily contrived just before Parker had entered the room. Evans reported to the two navy men that a prominent Soviet official had requested asylum in exchange for a large amount of highly sensitive military data. This operative demanded that he be extricated within the next seven days or the deal is off. The agency would normally do a "switch" where their man would exchange identity documents with the Russian. The defector would exit immediately using these papers while the agent would be casually moved to Berlin for transit to the Western Sector. Orin Ellsworth, Parker's replacement, could be flown in early but he had no field experience. The consensus was that Parker had shown enough talent to do the job. Besides, they desperately needed Ellsworth as a long-term agent. From the start, Parker had been categorized as expendable. No strong family ties and no strings tying him to any ongoing covert action. If anything went wrong, his absence would hardly cause a ripple.

They agreed that because of the risks, Parker could not be ordered to take this assignment. Someone had to con him into accepting it. Smythe lost the toss of the coins. They would set Parker up during the Kocise debriefing up by announcing his return to the prosaic assignment on the Destroyer and see how he reacted. If he took a psychological dive, maybe they could catch him at the bottom; tempt him with one last assignment. It was a long shot, but they were desperate.

James watched Airy slip into a midnight blue evening gown that looked like it came right out of Vogue. Before he could catch his breath, she asked him to clasp a necklace that perfectly accented the dress.

"Did you rob Selfridges?" he asked.

"Just about. I told Mr. Harrington that you were introducing me to the Embassy staff tonight. He told me to take anything I wanted for tonight. I refused, but he insisted. I have to get everything back by Monday morning. Sort of like Cinderella."

"You're not having an affair with Harrington, are you?"

'The thought did pass my mind. Right now I'm just saving him for a back up in case things don't work out between you and me," she said without facing him.

"Hmmmm," was the best Parker could come up with.

The reception was more elaborate than Parker had expected. About 40 couples from both the British and American Embassies were present. Only Foxworthy appeared to be alone. The American Ambassador was along side a British Minister introducing a new attaché.

"Don't be nervous, Airy. These are all people I work with," James coached.

"I feel like I'm going to meet the Queen," Airy replied as they approached the Ambassador.

The Ambassador made the initial introduction. "This is Lieutenant Parker, our chief courier at the Embassy."

Parker was pleased by the meaningless promotion since he was the only courier.

"He's been doing a fine job for us," the Ambassador continued.

Parker nodded. "Let me introduce my companion, Miss Airy Reynolds."

They made a stunning entrance to the main hall. Chad came over trailing the exotic Catherine, but the pair was trumped by the formal Navy White Uniform against a perfectly formed Royal Blue silhouette.

"Well, this is a pleasant surprise," Chad said eager to introduce Catherine.

Airy smiled and extended her gloved hand to Chad. "Charmed," she countered.

"Airy, this is Catherine. You remember Parker."

"Yes, the file clerk."

Parker winced. "It's a private joke, Airy," he tried to explain.

The American staff all took turns chatting with Airy who impressed them with her quick and congenial replies. Her experience working with people at Selfridges was paying off in cementing British-American relationships that evening.

Sunday was a special day for Airy.

"It's our fifth anniversary. Five months today!" Airy smiled as she bent over to light the single candle on the kitchen table. She had sweet-talked the butcher into saving a lamb roast for her. It was a very special occasion. She had never before been in a serious relationship. "I'm happy the Embassy let you move in, even if it's only for ten days."

"Here's to the five greatest months of my life," James said as he raised his wineglass as in a toast. "I don't know if I can get used to being idle for ten straight days. Maybe I can come down to Selfridges and load merchandise onto the shelves."

"Absolutely not! I want you to rest. You're going to need all the energy you can muster."

He grabbed her arm and drew her into his lap kissing her tenderly. They kissed again. Blood rushed to his organs as he felt her grow more supple. His hand brushed over her blouse. She was not wearing a brassier. It was a turn on signal they had developed over the five months. He swept her up in his arms; their lips never parted as he carried her through the kitchen headed towards the bedroom. Airy motioned with her free hand towards the stove without drawing back her lips. She grabbed the roaster cover and as Parker spun her around she dropped it over the roast.

The first two days were ecstasy. Airy consumed him in the evenings and he could loaf all day. But on the third day reality began to set in. There was nothing to do. The quick change of pace started to chafe his nerves. He called in daily, but there were no messages. He had to do something. He knew Foxworthy took a run each day so he bought a pair of sneakers and he plotted a course to intercept him at the midpoint of his route.

"Where the hell did you come from?" Foxworthy shouted as Parker appeared at his side as he made the turn at the northeast corner of Hyde Park.

"Just trying to get a little exercise," he responded trying to keep in stride with Foxworthy. "Nice day."

"Any day it doesn't rain in London is a nice day."

"Anything new on my replacement?" Parker queried. He tried to make the words come out casually, but they came out in puffs.

"Everything's on schedule, Lieutenant. Ever do much running?"

"A little. I went to the same high school as Jesse Owens."

"Well, that won't get you much here. Try getting yourself a decent pair of running shoes."

Foxworthy turned up the pace until Parker dropped out.

"What are you doing here? You're supposed to be on vacation," Chad said as he grabbed his tray in the lunch line.

"I'm doing all the cooking and laundry at the flat. I need a break. Airy can't get any time off now with the Christmas stock starting to come in, and BBC isn't worth a shit during the day." Parker grabbed a tray and fell into line.

"I understand your replacement had high marks at the farm," Chad casually mentioned. "Ivy League background, I hear."

"Well you know me. I'll probably be teletyping for your help to tell port from starboard when I get back to the ship. Keep the reply Top Secret, will you. How's the Russian connection doing?"

"They've asked me to lay off for awhile. They're afraid she's trying to blow my cover." He paused for a reaction. "That was a joke, Parker. It's classified."

"Airy wants to know how her visa is coming along."

"It's not going to be easy. We're checking on her sister in the states right now."

When Foxworthy finished his morning run, he went directly to his office and picked up the phone.

"Smythe. He's ready, call him in. We have to know today or we miss the window."

He hung up without waiting for an answer. He needed a good long shower.

Smythe's office was a mess as usual. He had just related to Parker the situation with the potential Russian defector. He paused to dunk his scone into his cup of coffee, but managed only to overflow the cup onto his desk.

"This mission is definitely not routine but a switch needs to be made now," he said as he tried to wipe up the coffee with a tissue.

Parker leaned forward. "What's the plan and what's a switch?"

"The Russian will be in Leningrad Wednesday. You will use the Swedish passport to arrange an overnight ferry from Stockholm to Leningrad on the premise of combining fun on the ferry ride with picking up some duty free vodka. Rent a modest cabin. The ferry spends about 5 hours in Leningrad. You will take the standard Intourist city tour. It always goes to the Hermitage Museum. The stop will be short since they are still under reconstruction. The tour will have time in the Palace Square to shop the street vendors. At the southwest entrance there is a group that has a dancing bear. They charge for being photographed with the bear. The contact will be there. You will have the same hat and overcoat. A few changes will be made in your appearance to match his as best we can. While the bear is performing, you slip the passport and tour documents to him in the crowd. Hence 'the switch.' He joins the tourist group, returns to the ship, and gets to Stockholm where we meet him."

"And I become a Russian citizen and live happily ever after?"

"You will take a taxi to a safe house in Leningrad. They will make arrangements for you to be taken by motor car to East Berlin. There we will have your uniform and papers to cross you into West Berlin. A flight to London should have you back by Sunday at the latest."

"There's got to be a catch here," Parker said.

There was a pause.

"Your status while in Russia is tenuous. You will be an illegal, a person who has no passport or any other record of entry into that country. You can't go to the Embassy. They couldn't legalize you without compromising the switch."

"In other words, if discovered, I'd be a spy and be shot."

"Most likely not. We've uncovered Russian illegals in the States and just sent them back. We rarely place an illegal in Russia, but if one were caught, we'd expect them to return the courtesy."

"I don't think I'd do well in Siberia. I hate cold weather."

"Look, Parker, we need to place someone in Leningrad Wednesday or there is no deal. We feel you have shown enough initiative to pull this off, and frankly there is no one else available on such short notice. But because of the high risk you can refuse if you don't think you can do it."

"Have you done anything about security here at the Embassy? That Copenhagen drop was too close for comfort."

"Only Evans, Foxworthy, and I are in on this. You'll have some contact with Higgins, but he knows nothing about the details of the mission. I will arrange transportation to Stockholm myself so there is no tie in to a travel agency. There won't be any leaks."

"I don't know. Too much risk versus reward."

There was quiet in the room until Smythe added, "We could arrange for a permanent visa for Airy immediately."

"Let me think about it. I'll sleep on it and tell you tomorrow."

Smythe broke in; "I need your answer now, before you leave the room."

CHAPTER TWENTY

Airy was not happy to say the least.

"I thought you were through with all that courier mish-mush."

"It's just three days. They guaranteed me at least two days here before I fly back to the Med."

"It's not fair."

"Airy, it's just routine. Besides, they promised to expedite a permanent visa. It should be approved before I return."

Airy rushed over to Parker. "I love you, Jimmy." She kissed him full on the lips.

The topcoat was heavy. The suit was of fair quality but rumpled. The tie was black and reminded him of funeral attire.

"Is the Embassy going to have a hard times party?" Higgins chuckled.

"Spare me the laughs, Chief."

"Try the shoes on. Maybe you remember them from your last trip. I thought you'd appreciate comfortable shoes. Sort of a personal touch. From me."

Parker didn't appreciate what he interpreted as sarcasm. He didn't want to tip his hand about the mission, so he didn't respond. Higgins was on the bottom of his mole-suspect list, but he couldn't take any chances. The shoes were comfortable and gave him a good feeling.

"I might buy these from you," Parker quipped.

The salt spray felt good on his face as Parker leaned over the rail of the Stockholm to Leningrad ferry. He pulled his overcoat around him to seal off the early autumn sea breeze. His hat was pulled down tight over his head.

Even Airy wouldn't have recognized him. His hair and even his eyebrows were dyed black. A mustache had been added with spirit gum and some putty changed the shape of his nose. Parker didn't like black. To him it was an ill omen on a mission that rested so heavily on chance. It gave him second thoughts, but it was too late to back out now.

While most of the passengers were reveling in cheap vodka, Parker confined himself to his small cabin. He signed up for the city tour, but avoided contact with the other passengers. With a Swedish passport and no command whatsoever of that language, he tried to remain obscure.

The city tour members assembled on the dock early the next morning. The director was obviously asking the languages preferences for the tour. Most of the hands went up for Swedish. Parker decided to keep his hands in his pockets. A sole hand went up for English and he released a stored breath. The Englishman was stout and was bent over with age requiring a cane. Maybe his luck was changing for the better.

Parker purposely entered the bus late and took a seat by himself. The tour director droned on in Swedish pointing out historical sites along the way, giving only a few words in English. "We will stop at the Astoria Hotel to use their toilets. Then we will visit our famous Hermitage." Most of the tourists were busy with their cameras. The Englishman sat stoically.

Nearly all of the artifacts had been removed from the Hermitage before the Germans began their 900-day siege of the city in 1942. The building itself escaped major damage and the exhibits were in the process of being returned. The tour director spent a lot of time pointing out what the still missing items were, but the grandeur of the building alone was worth the visit. Upon exiting, the director gave instructions in Swedish, then added in English. "We must stay together, so follow me around the square."

The square is actually round. The group headed left towards the east entrance to start a clockwise route. Parker tensed up as they headed straight for the Russian bear act. It had attracted the largest group of tourists. As they approached, his heart began to race. He could see a figure with a similar hat well into the crowd. His hand, wet with perspiration, grasped the black folder containing the passport and the return ferry ticket. Moving as quickly as he could, he threaded his way toward the hat. The dark blue overcoat matched his. The face was older, but the hair, eyebrows, mustache, and even the nose were passably close to his. They made eye contact and the switch was on. The folder was passed effortlessly between them. Parker moved away and joined a half dozen other tourists who were headed back towards the Hermitage.

As the distance between them increased, Parker turned for a moment and caught a glimpse of the Russian. He was walking away with the group. Close by him was the Englishman. They were talking. Either the Russian was establishing a friend to vouch for him if necessary, or the Englishman was part of the plan that Parker was not privy to. It was no longer his concern. He was on his own. An illegal, a man without a country, a spy to be shot at dawn. He quickened his step breaking off from the group. Taxis were scarce, but he spied one at the corner and jumped into the front seat next to the driver.

"Speak English?" Parker asked holding out a matchbook

"You have luck, comrade," the taxi driver said proudly. "Aleks only taxi driver in Leningrad speak English good," he added pointing to himself.

It wasn't good, but good enough. Parker opened the matchbook and showed Aleks the address of the safe house written inside. "I have a cousin who just moved here," he said. In seconds, the taxi spun around and headed south. Black smoke poured out of the exhaust pipe as if to lay down a smoke screen that would magically hide them from any pursuers.

"You are American, no?"

"I was an American," Parker replied making up a story. "I've got Swedish citizenship now and work in Stockholm."

"I drive Americans in 1946. They look for trucks and jeeps they sent during war. You know how many they find?"

Parker wasn't interested, but he didn't want to offend the driver. "No, how many did they find?"

"None, *niskolko, nol*. They ask me, Aleks, where are all the trucks and jeeps we sent Russia? You know what I tell them?"

Parker grunted.

"I tell them Stalin has them in Moscow. I tell them they so good Stalin want make them tanks for army."

"How far to my cousin's house?"

"Soon, about two kilometers."

Parker looked at the driver. He was young, probably missed seeing any service during the war. Obviously he was smart enough to pick up English. "Do you earn much money driving a taxi?"

"The motherland owns the taxi. I keep the tips," he replied with a smile. "Two more blocks, straight ahead. Do you know why the taxi's are painted yellow?"

Parker dreaded another riddle. Before he could reply, the Aleks made a sharp right turn swinging Parker into his lap. The taxi slowed.

"Your cousin, is he in drugs?" the driver asked anxiously.

"He's a book salesman." Parker straightened himself in the seat. "What's wrong?"

"There's two KGB Volgas in front of his house. I know those cars. Your cousin is in big trouble." Aleks continued right turns until he crossed the intersection again to look down the street. The cars were still there.

"Drive away," Parker commanded. He slouched trying to disappear into his seat. He needed time to think.

Aleks drove north for a block, then stopped and hailed a pedestrian. They spoke rapidly in Russian. Aleks waved, then drove off. "There was KGB raid. I think you should get out now." He stopped the taxi.

"I think I would like to rent your taxi for the day," Parker answered. He shifted his weight slowly taking his wallet out, pulling out an American twenty-dollar bill, and placed it on the driver's knee.

Aleks looked at the money. On the black market it would fetch more rubles than he made in a month. He then looked at Parker. "How do you know that I won't take money and turn you over to KGB?"

"How do you know that I won't put a bullet through your head if you give me any more crap?"

The driver laughed nervously and cautiously picked up the money.

CHAPTER TWENTY ONE

Aleks was having the time of his life. Parker picked up the lunch tab at the best restaurant that the Russian could select where they would not attract attention. In turn, his tour of Leningrad taught Parker more about Russian history than he wanted to know. The highlight of the tour was the naval cruiser Aurora that fired the shot signaling the peasant assault on the Palace in 1917. The two men were within a few years of the same age and exchanged stories. Aleks told of being too young to be conscripted in the army, yet firing a rifle in defense of Leningrad during the siege. Parker told some sea stories about his experiences on a small patrol craft in the Pacific. He was more fortunate than Aleks. The atomic bomb ended the war before he saw any action. As the day waned, they had developed a special kinship. Parker felt he could take a chance and level with Aleks. Besides, he was running out of options.

"I need a place to stay for one night, Aleks. What can you do?"

"There is many good hotels I can take you."

Parker shook his head.

"Are they look for you?"

"No, it's not that. My papers are not in order. I need some time to straighten them out. Can you put me up at your place?"

Aleks laughed. "In Leningrad we are five, six in one flat. Only one bath on floor. No." Aleks paused, scratching his head. "Maybe I call in, report breakdown. You sleep in taxi." He held his hand out.

Two more twenties came out of Parker's wallet.

Aleks pulled his taxi to the rear of a giant apartment building. Parker went to the back seat as the Russian jacked up the left rear side, removed the tire, and placed it in the front seat. He would call in and say he broke down. Aleks waved and disappeared into the building. Parker felt abandoned: by the CIA, by the U.S. Navy, by Aleks, and maybe by God himself. He pulled his coat tightly around his body and shivered. It wasn't just from the cold.

Cramped in the back seat of the taxi overnight, Parker stretched to get a better position as the early morning sun added some measure of warmth to the vehicle. He had dreamed of Airy. He could even see her now, at the breakfast table gazing at him over a cup of steaming tea.

The car door rattled. The vision of Airy burst with a rush of reality. No one could be looking for him yet. The Russian could have barely made it to Stockholm. Trying to disappear inside a small taxi was out of the question, so Parker slowly righted himself to face his adversary. It was a small boy with a backpack. Probably just a curious schoolboy. Parker played his game. He smiled and waved. The boy lost interest and walked away.

The door at his back opened abruptly and Parker almost fell out backwards, catching himself just in time. Aleks grinned.

Parker was not in a humorous mood. "You scared the shit out of me. Let's get out of here right now."

"I need change one twenty to rubles to show fare then take taxi to garage," Aleks said as he began replacing the tire. "I drop you off quick."

The cold and hunger dulled his wits. Parker needed time to think. "The safest place for both of us is the Hermitage where you picked me up."

The ten minute ride to the Palace Square was enough for Parker to sketch out an escape plan. The worst thing he could do was stay in Leningrad too long. Once the defection was discovered, they would be looking for the accomplice. One of the maps he used in Norway included Sweden and Finland. He remembered how close Leningrad was to Finland. The swampy border could be crossed on trains or roadways. Once there the Embassy should have no trouble bailing him out. The brakes on the taxi screeched as it came to a stop. Parker stepped out and he waved as the taxi turned, hoping that the brief friendship would at least buy him a few more hours of freedom.

The Astoria Hotel was only a few blocks away. Yesterday's tourist stop convinced him that he would not be as conspicuous there as at other hotels. He headed towards the public toilets, having the necessary rubles in hand as he approached. A wrinkled-faced attendant took the money and pointed him in the correct direction.

The lone mirror in the men's room showed Parker's naturally light colored stubble was hardly noticeable. He removed the mustache and the putty from his nose. If Aleks gave him up, at least those

219

changes might throw them off. The reasonable reflection gave him the inspiration to try a bold approach, at least for breakfast. After all, if they were looking for him they wouldn't expect him to be having breakfast with a window seat at the Astoria. Besides he was very hungry.

The eggs Benedict were settling in. Parker was relaxing with his second cup of coffee. His view of the people rushing to work with a purpose reminded him that he needed a purpose, a plan. He had to gamble. The only hint of a contact in Leningrad was the bear act. If the carni man in Copenhagen was in on the drop, maybe the gypsies running the bear act were somehow on the payroll.

It was almost noon when Parker returned to the Palace Square. The gypsies were just getting the bear in place and were setting up the music box. A couple seemed to be in charge. He recognized the man from yesterday. Parker looked at him, but the man avoided eye contact. "Nice bear," Parker spoke in a monotone as if it were a recognition code.

The man tilted his head. "You want buy food to feed bear?"

Parker nodded and cautiously handed him a twenty.

The gypsy looked at the money, then looked up at Parker. "Twenty dollars feed the bear for month. You want buy bear?"

A decision had to be made quickly before the square filled with tourists. "Someone stole my passport. I need to get to Helsinki, but cannot contact any Embassies. Can you help?"

"Have you money?"

"Yes"

The gypsy turned towards the bear and waved to the man and woman grooming it. "Trinka." he beckoned. The woman came towards them. As they talked intently in Russian, Parker was wary of becoming conspicuous.

"I'm Alexei," the gypsy said extending his hand. "This is my wife Trinka. She speaks little English. We go to small fair in Finland tomorrow. We take you for $100. From there you go to Helsinki yourself."

Parker nodded acceptance. His luck seemed to be holding.

Alexei pointed towards the bear. "You take Issac's place. Trinka show you where change clothes with him."

They walked back to the bear. Alexei grabbed the bear's muzzle and pointed it towards Parker.

"What is your name, comrade?"

"Smith," Parker replied without hesitation.

"Smith meet Balzac. You two good friends, no?"

The bear snorted.

Trinka led Parker and Issac to a small truck used to haul the bear. Issac spoke no English, but Trinka made it clear to him what was going on. They were both about the same size so the exchange went smoothly. As Parker stripped down he suddenly felt naked without a holster and gun. On second thought, the gun would have been useless. He needed friends, not weapons.

Issac, pleased with the trade, left the truck and disappeared down the street. Trinka led the way back to the bear. A small crowd started to gather.

"What does Issac do?" Parker asked.

"Clean up after bear."

Balzac was a Russian Brown Bear about six feet tall and 400 pounds. He was captured as a cub and raised by Alexei and Trinka. They trained him to do an act which allowed them to earn a meager living but provided them with a means of getting around the country without a lot of formalities. Smuggling was their main occupation. Alexei worked the crowd with card games while Trinka told fortunes. Issac, Trinka's brother, was there to take care of Balzac.

The heavy scent of Issac from the clothes Parker now wore made the bear feel at ease.

"Keep a tight rein and keep muzzle on," Alexei warned. "I feed him meat. You feed him grain."

"He seems to like me," Parker said.

"I show you trick," Alexei responded. "KGB!" The bear roared and jumped up and down.

A few miles outside of town, the truck turned off the road onto a dirt path. It swayed over the rocky terrain until a small hut appeared in an opening where it came to an abrupt stop. Alexei looked back in the truck. Parker was propped up next to the bear cage.

"We stay here tonight. You sleep with Balzac. Become good friends."

It was another cold night for Parker. He wished he could have kept the overcoat, which now was warming Issac. He reflected how stupid he was to take this assignment when he could have been in bed with Airy feeling the warmth of her soft body. He was frightened he would be captured, but even more frightened that he would never see Airy again. Damn it! Damn it! Damn it!

CHAPTER TWENTY TWO

Ivan burst into Chernoff's office wildly waving a paper.

"Urgent message, Comrade. Deputy Minister of Armament Josef Smolski has been reported missing."

Chernoff snatched the message from Ivan and continued to read. "He was reported on his way to visit to his sister in Leningrad, but he never arrived. All border crossings have been given photos and instructions." The message hinted strongly of defection. An official of this high ranking crossing over would be more than just an embarrassment to the Motherland. God only knows what secrets he has in his head.

Chernoff crumpled the message in his hand and walked to the window. It all came together for him. The London agent reported yesterday that Parker had a ticket to Stockholm. There had to be a connection. He must be a key figure in what was appearing to be a major defection.

"Get the photo of Parker," Chernoff barked, "and send it to all the border crossings into Finland and East Berlin. Mark him as extremely dangerous. Note to have all sightings reported direct to my office. Get his photo to the custom officials on boats traveling to and from Leningrad. See if anyone recognized him. If Parker is in Russia, we will catch him."

Ivan turned to go, then paused. "Do you think its possible that Parker escorted him out of the country?"

"Let me do the thinking, Comrade. Get that photo on the wire. When you've done that, come back. I need to send a letter to Moscow."

* * *

It was a cold Leningrad morning. Every breath was visible. Alexei had made an early start heading north. The roads were in terrible condition and each hole or bump was a shock wave to be reckoned with. Parker was seated on the truck bed with no padding. Even Balzac was restless.

With the border crossing in sight, the truck slowed. Alexei roused Trinka from her dozing then partially turned toward the small window separating the cab from the truck bed. "Smith, say nothing. The guards know us."

Three Russian soldiers were at the barrier. Alexei recognized two of them and gave a friendly wave. The gate went up, but the third soldier, a corporal, came over and took a long look at the gypsy garb worn by Alexei and Trinka.

"Open the truck for inspection, Comrade."

The other two soldiers stood back. They were obviously outranked.

Alexei got out and went to the rear.

"We are a traveling show on our way to Lappeenranta to take some money from the Finnish peasants."

The corporal was not to be put off. "Open the truck."

Parker, hearing the conversation but not understanding, knew he was in for some kind of trouble. When he heard the door being unlatched, he leaned toward Balzac.

"KGB," Parker commanded Balzac just as the door was opening. The timing was perfect. The bear roared and jumped up and down not a meter from the corporal who jumped back and let out a yelp. The other two guards doubled with laughter as Alexei quickly closed the doors.

They were still laughing when the truck passed the barrier.

A half-hour later a messenger on a bicycle handed a package to the guard house at the Nuijamaa crossing. The corporal opened the package and pulled a bulletin containing photos of Parker and Smolski. Without hesitation he called the priority number at the bottom of the notice, then summoned the two privates. When he finished his tirade, they were not laughing.

The location for the bear act was critical for the gypsies to make money at the fairground. Alexei was bargaining hard for a favorable site on the fairway for maximum exposure. The bear was only a diversion for the crowd. The real money today would be made with card and shell games performed between acts. Trinka would do her best to foretell fortunes to the eager Finns for a price. On this trip they would have to forego Issac's talents as an expert pickpocket, but they were already 100 US dollars ahead which was more than a week's work. Picking up goods to be smuggled across the border would come after the weekend.

It was late in the morning before the arrangements were finally concluded. The crowd was expected around noon. Various vendors were setting up their stalls anticipating a good day since the weather was dry, if not sunny.

Parker had just removed Balzac from his cage and tied him to a nearby tree. He returned to clean out the cage which had become his routine. His mind was buzzing with the next step of his plan to get to Helsinki without drawing attention to himself. He would ask Alesei to point out vendors who may be headed to Helsinki when the fair closes. In the meantime he would just do his work and stay out of sight.

A large black Russian car arrived at the fairground entrance. The driver leaned out his window to exchange a few words with a passerby. The car rapidly swung crosswise blocking the roadway to the fairground. Before Parker could react, two men got out of the car and walked rapidly towards Alexei's truck. They spotted Parker and ran directly towards him. He dropped his broom and headed for Balzac. If he could release the bear, he might have a chance. It was too late. They reached him first and grabbed both arms and lifted him off the ground. Parker shouted, "KGB! KGB!" Balzac dutifully roared and jumped up and down. The bear could have easily snapped the leash, but made no attempt to break loose. For him it was just part of the act.

Inside the car Parker was pinned between the two men.

"You can't do this!" Parker shouted. "This isn't Russia!"

The man on his right pulled something out of his coat pocket and struck Parker just at the frontal hairline. He slumped in his seat. Blood streamed down his face.

CHAPTER TWENTY THREE

Finland had the unique experience of fighting the Russians twice during World War II and ending up losing both times. As Germany devoured Austria, Czechoslovakia, and then Poland by October 1939, Russia looked hungrily to recover the disputed territory of Karelia. This area just north of Leningrad that was awarded to Finland in 1921 by the League of Nations and was considered to be a gnawing insult to Mother Russia. On November 30, 1939 Russia marched into Finland and began the "Winter War" to redress this grievance.

The Finns initially put up strong resistance and stopped the Soviet advance towards the higher elevations. Photographs of Finnish soldiers on skis, almost invisible in the snow wearing their white coveralls were splashed on the pages of Life and Look magazines. The Russians, poorly equipped for winter mountain warfare, were easy targets. Press stories of the David-Goliath match up made the front pages, but brought no help for the Finns. The fact that tiny Finland was the only country that made regular payments of its debts to the United States from WWI was insufficient to sway the American isolationists. Not a single package of American supplies ever reached Finland.

The shear weight of numbers finally prevailed and Finland surrendered in March 1940. As part of the armistice agreement, Finland ceded port facilities for a naval base in Hango on the southwestern coast.

When the Germans invaded Russia on June 22, 1941, the Finns saw this as an opportunity to turn the tables on the Russians. They provided access for the Germans and aided them in their attack on Leningrad from the north, retaking Karelia. But the Soviets took their revenge in 1944 when the siege of Leningrad was lifted. On September 19 a second armistice was signed, returning Karelia to Russia. Experience told the Russians that Finland was not worth the hassle of occupation. To insure that the Finns would know who their masters were, the Russians occupied a desolate peninsula just south west of Helsinki. The Soviets dredged a harbor in an area called Porkkala and set up a naval base. A fence was constructed across the peninsula and for all practical purposes this promontory became part of the Soviet Union.

The car containing the semi-conscious Parker approached the gate to Porkkala. The guards looked inside briefly and then flagged the car through.

"So, what is it? Are you Parker or Smith?" Commissar Bolstoy asked as he towered over the seated captive. Bolstoy was a key official in the Communist Party. He was a large man who relished being in total charge of the Porkkala complex. He had a comfortable home built on the peninsula some distance away from the wharf area. His responsibilities were simple: Security and maintenance of the piers for the occasional warship that pulled in. He took his work seriously and demanded strict obedience to orders.

The room was void of furniture except for the single chair Parker was sitting on. Two Russian guards stood behind the Commissar.

"We know you are Parker. We have your photo. Admit it!"

Parker's head throbbed. He wasn't sure where he was, only that he had been unconscious for a long time. The cold and now the fear impeded his ability to concentrate. He could only think of taking refuge in the Geneva Convention.

"Parker, United States Navy, Lieutenant, 297-16-47."

"You are lieutenant SHIT!" Bolstoy screamed, then paused to gain some degree of composure.

"Where is your uniform, Lieutenant?" Bolstoy taunted. "Where are your papers?" He began to rave. "You are a spy and I will take pleasure in ordering your execution!"

Parker remained silent.

"Let's see if I can help you remember more than just your serial number." He raised his left foot and jammed Parker's two smallest fingers on his right hand against the wooden arm of the chair. They cracked like dry autumn twigs.

At first, surprise blocked out the pain, but that lasted only for a second. He stared down at his fingers. They were broken but there was no blood. The pain was excruciating and he gasped for breath as panic began to set in.

The Russian officer spun around sweeping his right hand towards the prisoner. The back of his gloved hand struck the Parker's face with a force that nearly knocked him off his chair. Blood trickled from his mouth.

"You are an American spy! Admit it," the Russian shouted as he brought his face close to the man. "Confess and you might be able to save yourself."

Parker sat on a wooden chair in the middle of the interrogation room. A solitary light shone down on him. It was cold and he was shirtless. He shook off the blow and looked up at his adversary.

"Lieutenant James C. Parker, United States Navy, 247 15….."

The Russian swung viciously with his other hand. This time Parker was able to turn his head slightly to mute the blow.

"Don't give me any more of that God damned Geneva Convention shit!" Bolstoy's eyes blazed as he grabbed Parker's hair and straightened him up. He brought his own face within inches of the prisoner's. His breath was coming in short bursts. He began speaking in staccato like tempo. "You were not in uniform when you were discovered! You have no papers. You are in a foreign country. This makes you a spy. We can shoot you anytime we want. Now, what was your mission? Who was your contact?" He raised his right hand as if to strike another blow.

Parker closed his eyes and shook his head. The Russian lowered his hand and motioned with his head. Two soldiers stepped forward out of the darkness.

"Perhaps you need a little more encouragement," the Russian said sarcastically as he released his grip and motioned to the soldiers. One placed his arm around the prisoner from behind clasping him to the chair. The other grabbed his right hand and unfolded his fingers. "Shall we break another finger?' The two smaller fingers already hung baroquely. The soldier grabbed the middle finger and slowly began to bend it back.

"I know nothing! They told me nothing. I am just a courier, a messenger," Parker pleaded. Fear mounted inside his brain and made him sick. He wanted to vomit, but nothing would come out. He had neither food nor water for the six hours since he had been taken prisoner. He had tried to keep his mind clear, but everything was starting to blur.

The officer motioned for the soldier to continue. A sharp crack resonated in the bare room. Parker screamed as the pain shot through his arm. He started to lose consciousness.

"Now, you are ready to tell me everything, no? I want to hear everything. Start from the beginning."

Parker wanted to say something but no words came out. His eyes started to glaze over, but *Start from the beginning* began to repeat in his brain as all else darkened. His body went limp and the soldiers had to hold him on the seat.

Trying to regain some semblance of consciousness, Parker repeatedly blinked his eyes. The image of Bolstoy was clear but the borders were hazy and dark.

"What were you doing in Leningrad?"

No answer.

"Why were you with the gypsies?"

Parker couldn't even think of plausible answer for that one.

Bolstoy's patience abandoned him. He moved forward.

"What were your orders?"

He raised his hand to strike Parker a third time when the door opened. Parker kept his gaze on Bolstoy.

"Your call to Berlin has gone through, Comrade Commissar."

Bolstoy snorted in disgust and left the room.

The pause in the inquisition gave Parker time to think. Maybe he wasn't back in Russia. The words "in a foreign country" rather than "here in Leningrad" gave him hope. While captive in the car, he had brief moments of consciousness. The road was smooth. The road to Leningrad was rough and full of potholes.

"Yes, Comrade Chernoff, we have Parker in custody now and are questioning him," Bolstoy spoke with authority into the phone. Capturing a spy would be noted as a major accomplishment in his personnel file. "We have arranged a military transport plane to fly you to Helsinki. My chauffeur will pick you up at the airport."

"Has he said anything yet?" Chernoff asked.

"Nothing so far, but we are just starting."

"Hold up on interrogation until I arrive. I want to hear any information he has directly, understood?"

"Yes, Comrade." Bolstoy was disappointed. He knew he could break Parker and take credit for a detailed confession ready upon Chernoff's arrival. They could then celebrate their triumphs with a glass of vodka and a good meal but he dared not disobey a command. He resigned himself to share the honors that accompany catching a spy.

During the six hours it took Chernoff to arrive, Parker was left in the room without food, water, or communications. Bolstoy wanted to be sure he would be ready to talk. Parker had time to think. He must still be in Finland, but where? If he knew where, perhaps he could escape somehow and still make it to Helsinki. If he were in Russia, he was doomed.

His desperation then turned to anger. He didn't like being slapped around by bullies. He was cold, hungry, and his fingers ached badly. He didn't like that either. He stalked around the room to get his blood circulating. For some measure of revenge, he took time to urinate in each corner of the room.

As the door to the cell rattled, Parker took the seat and feigned a stupor. Two guards came in and roughly positioned the chair with Parker so that he faced the bare wall, his back to the door. He heard multiple footsteps, then the door closed.

"Well, Lieutenant Parker, it's time you told us all about your little escapade in Leningrad," Bolstoy began smoothly. "And don't give us any more of that Geneva Convention crap. You are technically a spy."

Parker remained silent.

"Perhaps you need a little more encouragement, Lieutenant." Bolstoy motioned for the guards to approach Parker. "Start with the small finger on his left hand."

There was no use playing hero any longer. The Russian defector was most certainly in England by now. "I'm just a courier. I was under orders to deliver some identification papers to another person at the

Palace square and switch places. I didn't know the identity of the person."

"You lie poorly, Lieutenant. You knew that it was a high official trying to defect. Who were your contacts in Leningrad?"

Parker hesitated for a moment too long. Before he could reply, Bolstoy signaled the guards and they repeated their maneuver slowly bending back the finger on the left hand.

"I never…made contact…in Leningrad. The safe house…. it was raided….before I got there. I know nothing. I'm just a courier….who…does…what…he is told."

The soldiers paused.

"More lies, Lieutenant. You know much more. Tell us about the gypsies. We want the names of your contacts in Leningrad." Bolstoy motioned the guards to continue their ritual.

"That's enough, Comrade," Chernoff interrupted as he stepped forward out of the darkness. "He knows nothing of interest to us. We can better use him to teach the Americans not to try this again."

"But Comrade Chernoff, we need his contacts, his missions," Bolstoy pleaded.

"A Leningrad safe house was raided and we know who those people are. It is better that we shoot him as an example to the CIA of what happens to an illegal."

Parker still being held by the guards couldn't believe his ears. He became suddenly limp. He had fainted. The guards let Parker slip to the floor.

Chernoff looked down upon Parker. "He doesn't look like much of a spy to me," he said giving the body a firm kick and then turned to Bolstoy. "Get him into a car. We'll take him outside the gate where I will kill him myself." Bolstoy looked in disbelief. He would have rather continued to torture Parker, but Chernoff outranked him. "Get a shirt for him," Chernoff added as he started out of the room. "I don't want the American authorities to think we are savages."

CHAPTER TWENTY FOUR

The black Volga roared north from Porkkala. Parker was in the back between Chernoff and a guard with the chauffeur and another guard in the front seat.

Chernoff had borrowed a gun from Bolstoy. "It's a fine gun. Did you use this in the war?" Chernoff questioned.

"Yes, it was my personal companion all the way to Berlin," Bolstoy bragged.

"I will take good care of it. It will be used again to kill another enemy of the Motherland."

Bolstoy tried to smile, but couldn't. While he felt comfortable with the gun in combat, he had no taste for murder. He was glad to have Chernoff volunteer.

Chernoff opened the clip. It was full. "Good. I may have to shoot him more than once, just to make sure he's dead. We don't want him to involve Palkkala, do we?"

The road beyond the illuminated gate ran pitch-black two miles toward the north before it intersected with the main road to Helsinki. When Chernoff guessed they were near the half way point, he signaled the chauffeur to stop. The guard pulled Parker from the car. Chernoff had his gun pointed towards Parker's chest and motioned for the guard to get back into the car.

"Walk," Chernoff ordered as he pointed to the dense forest to his left. The overgrowth was thick as Parker, prodded by the pistol, stumbled forward. He was in no way ready to die, but. he knew his chances for survival were slim. What a shitty way to die, he thought. Tomorrow he'd be just another "lost" courier. He was sinking into hopeless despair.

"Listen to me, Parker," Chernoff started. "You are simply worthless. You and I know you are just a messenger. They kept you stupid and uninformed." He gave Parker another nudge with the pistol to keep him moving. "But killing you may be useful, after all."

Parker knew his death sentence when he heard it. Desperation closed in. He chose to die facing his killer, so he boldly stopped and turned to face Chernoff.

Chernoff pulled the trigger.

The flash was blinding to Parker, but he felt no pain. His legs gave way and he fell to the ground. So this is how you die, he thought. You die so quickly; you don't feel the pain. Then he heard a second shot. He wasn't dead after all. Both shots missed their mark.

Chernoff bent over Parker. "I saved your life, Parker. Now you are going to save mine. Stay here in the forest until dawn. Walk north to the highway. Hitch a ride East to Helsinki; the Finns pick up hikers. Go to the American Embassy. When you get to London, tell them I am ready to cross over. Run a personal ad in the London Times. Use DROP 9611. I'll be in Paris three days later."

He grabbed Parker's left hand and wrote something on the left palm with a pen.

Parker lay on the ground in disbelief. Before he could utter a sound, Chernoff had disappeared into the darkness.

The first order of business was to survive the night air. He felt around. The leaves had already fallen in abundance. He gathered up enough to form a bed and then proceeded to cover himself as well as he could. He silently thanked Chernoff for sparing his life and then for the shirt. He knew a person could easily survive without food and water for at least twenty-four hours. His youth would surely give him an extra twenty hours, but hypothermia was something else.

The leaves did their job and the rising sun provided enough heat to get him thinking. He looked in his pockets. The Russians had taken everything. He sat and stared at the only remaining things that he had started with, his shoes. Higgins had given him the same shoes he had in Slovakia. There must be a reason. They had been resoled. The right one looked bulkier than the left one. He scuffed its toe against a rock and the sole parted slightly from the shoe. He could see something green. Higgins had come through again, but he would have settled for a candy bar.

Parker started to walk in the direction of the sun. It took nearly an hour to break through the dense forest to the highway. He carefully chose his spot to beg for a ride. With a view along the highway, he picked a car that bypassed the turn to the peninsula. The first car stopped. When he showed the driver a twenty-dollar bill he had taken from the shoe, he had no problem in convincing the driver to take him directly to the American Embassy. He leaned back in his seat and looked at his right hand. Only his thumb and index finger would move. The pain in the other fingers, deadened by the tension of the past hours, was beginning to return. Fortunately none of the breaks ruptured the skin.

He opened his left hand. Something was written on his palm. He brought it closer to read in the morning sun. Printed in ink was DROP 9611.

CHAPTER TWENTY FIVE

The military transport aircraft taxied up to a VIP
gate at Heathrow. An Embassy car pulled on the
tarmac and Parker stepped directly from the plane's
gangway into the car. Smythe was in the car. The
heavily tinted windows shielded them from view.

"Welcome back to our little piece of America,"
Smythe greeted Parker. Noting Parker's bandaged right
hand, he discretely grabbed his right upper arm.

"What the hell went wrong in Leningrad? I came
within an inch of getting caught in that safe house
raid." Parker reinforced the comment with his
unbandaged left hand.

"You were right about that leak. Someone tipped
off the Ruskies. We just got Smolski out in time. When
we heard they raided the safe house, we thought you
were a goner. You were damn lucky to get out alive."
Smythe felt uneasy discussing the Embassies' failures
and wanted to change the subject. "I see the Finns
stitched up your forehead. Good thing it's inside the
hairline. How are the fingers?

"They reset them but they hurt like hell."

"Why don't you just rest. Evans and Foxworthy are
waiting. No sense repeating the story."

Smythe clandestinely brought Parker in through the
rear entrance of the Embassy. They headed toward
Foxworthy's office. A young Yeoman Third Class was
seated at Penelope's desk. The ballerina doll was
missing.

Parker told his story in detail. "I came this close to getting killed," he said pointing to the powder burns on his face from Chernoff's first shot.

"Amazing story," Evans commented. "We got Smolski out and you're back safe. That's a good mission."

"Sir," Parker said turning towards Foxworthy. "I need to call Airy. I'm three days overdue and she'll be worried sick."

"Afraid you can't contact Airy," Smythe interjected. "We don't want the Ruskies to know you made it back. So far as they are concerned, you are dead and we want to keep it that way. As soon as you clean up here, we're having the Military Air Transport Service take you to Naples. We've also made some revisions in your service jacket so tracing you will be difficult."

"Now wait one minute. I risk my hide to pull off a CIA stunt and you don't have the decency to let my fiancé know I'm alive!" Parker rose out of his chair. "You guys are nuts!"

"Parker," Foxworthy said in his best command voice. "Sit down. We need some time, that's all. Your assignment here is over. Airy has her visa to the States. Let us handle this. At the proper time we'll see that she gets to Pittsburgh and you can meet her there."

Parker sat down. He was still in the Navy. He had no other choice.

"We have a uniform for you in my office," Smythe said indicating the meeting was over.

As Parker got up to leave, he stopped and turned towards Evans. "It was Penelope, wasn't it?"

"Yes," Evans nodded.

"Shit. I thought sure it was Chad." He left shaking his head.

CHAPTER TWENTY SIX

The telephone rang. Airy looked at the bedroom clock. It was 7 am. She reached across Parker laying beside her to pick up the call.

"Yes. No, he's still sleeping."

Parker opened one eye.

"All right, I'll tell him. I'm sure he will. Oh? Well, I'll pass it on to him."

She replaced the phone and shook Parker. "Jimmy, don't pretend you're sleeping. Rodney Blair called in sick and Marge wants you to take his nine o'clock M150 class today."

"I hate that woman," Parker bellowed as he pulled the pillow over his head. Marge Cassidy was the Math Department Head at Erie State Community College. Department heads were considered the bottom feeders of the academic food chain. They got stuck with the job if they couldn't cut it as a full professor. "She sticks it to me every chance she gets."

He pulled Airy closer. "Let's take a plane somewhere and goof off for a month."

"Jimmy, behave yourself. You know you love your job."

Sensing Airy's rejection of his suggested odyssey, his feet hit the floor. "I still think a month off in some far away place is the right choice."

"By the way, Jimmy, she said you had a message."

"Oh?'

"Boris said he wants to meet you for lunch. For a language instructor, he is a total bore. I don't see what you two have in common."

Parker didn't answer.

Jack Petro

About the Author

Author Jack Petro saw Navy duty both as an enlisted man during World War II and as an officer during the Korean War. Much like his hero, James Parker, Petro was tapped for Naval Classified Material Courier duty. "No Ordinary Spy" is based on his own experiences and those of others during this assignment.

Petro worked at General, Electric where he managed several manufacturing facilities. In post retirement, he taught at a Junior College where he honed his writing skills

Currently Petro is an award winning Theater Critic covering live performances throughout North Central Florida. His column appears weekly in the Villages Daily Sun.

Printed in the United States
1252800001B/84